THE COMPLETE GUIDE TO LAW FIRM INTAKE

Powerful Strategies To Maximize Retention and Increase Revenue

Gary P. Falkowitz, Esq.

THE COMPLETE GUIDE TO LAW FIRM INTAKE

Powerful Strategies To Maximize Retention and Increase Revenue

ISBN-13: 978-1-946203-26-7

ISBN-10: 1-946203-26-2

Expert Press

www.ExpertPress.net

It amazes me how many firms do not understand the great financial impact of implementing and using high functioning new case intake procedures. Even small mistakes can cost your firm millions of dollars a year, no matter how many new case intakes you have each year. The problem is often the result of the belief that we are doing everything the best it can be done since that is the way we always did it. The fact is most firms have never had their intake process analyzed by someone with the skills of a new case intake professional – NEVER!! Times have changed – Big Time! And so has the level of your competition. There are real game-changing new case intake procedures the vast majority of law firms lack, which if implemented, will greatly enhance your firm's profitability, with little cost to the firm. Gary, by way of training he received running the intake department at Parker Waichman LLP and the systems he has learned since, has the ability to quickly analyze a firm's intake procedures and recommend and implement policies and procedures that will greatly improve your firm's profitability. I would not be surprised to see an increase in retained cases of 20% or more after Gary's suggestions are fully implemented. I highly recommend Gary to anyone who wants to see a dramatic increase in the percentage of new cases retained by their firm.

– Jerry Parker,
Owner at Parker Waichman LLP

Gary is a game changer! He truly "gets it" and provides a powerful but respectful outside voice. He has had a positive and dramatic impact on signed quality cases. We are only sorry we didn't find Gary earlier. Our brand and intake has never been stronger...thanks to Gary's valuable guidance and approach.

– David Gruber,
Owner at Gruber Law Offices LLC

There are few people I could recommend more highly than Gary. His understanding of the intake process and his ability to execute separate him from virtually anyone else in the field. Gary has an enthusiasm for intake, an area of most practices that is overlooked. If you've taken your intake for granted, I promise you that you don't know what you don't know. Intake is the most data driven area of any personal injury practice and it is only with intensity, training and dedication that you can uncover all the holes in your process and fill them so that you can be competitive in one of the world's most competitive business models. No matter how tight your intake process is, I can promise you that you are not as good as you think you are. Working with Gary has opened my eyes to the fact that without constant oversight along with policies and procedures in place to plug the holes, you will always be missing/ dropping cases and ultimately never be as profitable as you can be.

– Glen Lerner,
Owner at Glen Lerner Injury Attorneys

Gary was spot on with his intake recommendations. Gary partnered with our management team to do a deep dive into the capabilities of our department and our individual personnel. We then worked with Gary to organize the department and redo our procedures to maximize our intake process. We now chase all potential leads and make our sign-up appointments while the client is on his/ her initial call. Our conversion rate is up significantly for the second straight year. Gary is the best at what he does.

– Michael Rosenzweig,
Partner at Edgar Snyder & Associates, LLC

Table of Contents

Profits Start At Intake

Owning your own law practice can be one of the most challenging, time consuming, and rewarding career decisions you ever make. Owning a *highly profitable law practice with maximized returns* is taking this even one step further. The challenges, time commitment, risk tolerance, and rewards for owning this type of law practice require a unique set of skills. The minimum required skills include accountability, a desire to constantly improve (even when you're already successful), and financial wherewithal. And that's just to begin.

This process is certainly an arduous one, which is why it is that much sweeter when it pays off. Assuming you've secured your funding, hired your staff, created your brand, bought your vanity phone number, added content to your website, hired a web chat provider, employed an answering service (*see* www.intake.law) and, finally, opened your personal injury law firm, you're ready, right? Well… not so fast.

The first task to accomplish is to ensure that leads are being generated. While I would love to discuss with you the best ways or refer companies to assist you in this regard, for purposes of this book, I'm going to assume you already know them. I'm also going to assume that due to all your hard work and planning, the leads are beginning to roll in. This is a triumphant moment for any attorney. Trust me, I have my own law practice and I understand how good it feels when potential clients are interested in my legal services. Most attorneys believe that when your marketing efforts begin to generate strong leads, you get to focus on the main reason most attorneys attended law school to begin with—to practice law in the pursuit of justice by litigating cases.

But something I've discovered—first at the law firms I've worked at and later on at the many law firms I've consulted with—is that *what is required to start a personal injury law practice is never enough to sustain it.* More importantly, almost every law firm that requires marketing to prosper has a huge blind spot, which is making a direct, significant, and negative impact on its revenue. Hidden in the triumph of retaining clients and winning cases is an ugly truth: as an industry, personal injury attorneys are losing a tremendous amount of money due to unknown flaws in their intake process. Yet, they're successful anyway.

Before we go any further, I'd like for you to consider your law firm's current stream of revenue and, if you're completely satisfied with how your law firm is currently performing, there is no need to read further. However, if you are curious to explore whether areas of your intake process could use improvement, if you're looking to strengthen your brand and maximize revenue, and ultimately sustain longevity within the industry, then what you're about to read could have an immediate and extraordinary impact on the financials of your law practice.

For most personal injury attorneys, intake is the one aspect of a law firm that can easily be disregarded and forgotten—especially if you're already profitable. Generally speaking, most law firms just ask their support staff to pick up the phone when it rings and "complete an intake." And, if they put some thought into it, may give their staff a script on what they should say to potential clients. After that, it's every employee for himself. The reality is that many law firms treat the intake process as an afterthought. Come to think of it, they treat intake as if it's a guarantee; if the phone rings, it doesn't matter who you put on the phone. As long as the intake specialist, paralegal, or receptionist is friendly enough, they often assume that the potential client has already chosen to retain their law firm's services, simply because they called. Why do so many of us make this costly assumption? It is a red herring: if you're making this assumption, then it's not the only misleading assumption being made. After spending many years managing and overseeing the intake department of a prominent, national law firm and consulting with the intake departments of many others, I've witnessed firsthand how many misleading assumptions can be made and how they can negatively impact a law firm's stream of revenue.

To give a brief background about my experience in intake, I started in a law firm in a conventional role, litigating mass tort cases on behalf of claimants who were injured by defective medical devices or dangerous medications. As a litigator, I realized something that many attorneys probably already know. That is, once a client commits to and retains a law firm, they rarely seek to change counsel. Think about this for a moment because it's quite a bizarre statement. It doesn't matter how infrequently attorneys or paralegals stay in contact with their clients. It doesn't matter how long it takes for a case to resolve. It doesn't matter how rude an attorney might be. The fact is that claimants are generally willing to put up with a lot to avoid the process of finding a new attorney.

However, I realized more than just this one thing while litigating. The margins associated with a personal injury law firm are unlike anything I've ever seen or imagined. When I did the simple math of computing cost per acquisition, attorney's fees, and rates of resolving cases, *I couldn't help but wonder what it took to acquire clients and why a law firm wouldn't do everything in its power to acquire more.* I was fortunate enough to work for a very well respected and successful personal injury attorney. I remember having a brief conversation with him early on in my tenure about this very observation. After sharing the above thoughts with him, he gave me a look and rhetorically asked why else I thought he was spending so much money on marketing and advertising? That look stuck with me and always will. I also recall expressing an interest early on that, should an opportunity present itself whereby I could be more involved on the front-end of the law practice—at intake—I would be extremely interested.

As luck and determination would have it, I was promoted to managing attorney of the intake department shortly thereafter. I will forever be grateful for this opportunity and the experience that came with it. As managing attorney, I started to understand what the overwhelming majority of personal injury law firms disregarded inadvertently—*the massive impact that a highly functioning intake department and process could have, and how seldom it was truly being utilized, let alone optimized.* I was assigned to what I believe to be the most important aspect of any personal injury law firm—the intake process. In my experience, money can buy two out of the three things you need to have and sustain a highly profitable law practice with maximized returns: new leads and legal experience. But the third thing cannot be bought by money. What am I referring to? The ability to *consistently sign* a high percentage of qualified leads (that is, the ability to successfully intake a viable claim). As you read this book, you will see how high functioning *intake* is critical for personal injury law firms and is what I consider to be the lifeblood of a successful, sustainable law practice.

My responsibilities as managing attorney included maximizing the law firm's retention rate (also known as *conversion percentage*), expanding its referral business, strengthening its brand and reducing waste, among other things. Through my years of experience and in speaking with hundreds of attorneys around the country, I found a shocking number of problems that boiled down to one general issue. Quite simply, personal injury law firms are not as aggressive or attentive when responding, qualifying, following-up and signing potential clients, leading to lost retention opportunities and missed revenue. We, as an industry, are not implementing efficient and effective intake procedures, and we are not holding ourselves accountable to the intake process.

After improving almost every metric associated with running a successful intake department as managing attorney, I left on a mission to consult, educate and improve the intake processes of law firms nationwide. Now, you have to understand something. I was 30-something, with an obviously supportive wife and three children, and I had no safety net waiting for me on the other side of being an employee. But I just knew that there was a need in our industry for intake consulting services (*see* www.maxintake.com) and I was impassioned by my purpose. I also knew that I had the knowledge, first-hand experience, and expertise necessary to significantly improve the intake process, develop procedures, and solve any problems associated with intake at any given law firm. What I immediately observed as a consultant not only confirmed my suspicions—it showed me that intake problems are endemic in personal injury law firms and a lot worse than I expected. No matter how good attorneys may be at litigating cases, most law firms neglect their intake. And, by neglect, I mean completely disregard it. And why not? If a law firm is profitable without having to focus or dedicate resources to the intake process, it must be good enough, right? Not really.

Personal injury law is in some regards very different from other fields of law. Our ability to stay afloat and make money depends almost completely on how well we put ourselves out there—how well we advertise and how effectively we communicate to potential clients once they contact us. Unlike some other businesses, we are obligated by codes of ethical conduct which dictate that our clients must come to us. In other words, in most jurisdictions, we are not allowed to cold-call to procure clients. We cannot contact hospitals or ring doorbells in search of people who have been wronged and/or injured. The only true way to reach potential clients is through marketing and advertising efforts. There is no alternative. Employing a strong marketing campaign is essential to successfully advertising to potential clients and generating leads. But good advertising can be very expensive. And if you can invest in making sure the public knows who you are and what services you can provide, it behooves you to invest in making sure that your intake doesn't drop the ball when a potential client decides to contact you.

This becomes even more imperative when you appreciate that every lead you generate is a lead you paid for. Your advertising dollars are the reason the potential client contacted your law firm. You market yourself with the hopes that you'll sign qualified cases that can give you an astronomical return on your investment. But to get that return on your investment, your law firm must be retained. If I had to speculate, I would argue that in the current personal injury climate, on average, the approach (of lack of approach) most law firms take to intake causes them to miss out on at least 30 percent of their qualified leads. By so doing, law firms not only waste the money they invested on advertising, but they also forego the massive amount of potential revenue in attorney's fees they could be earning.

Whether one would admit it aloud or not, one of the most appealing aspects of owning a personal injury law practice is that the return on investment (you'll see this abbreviated as *ROI* in this book), compared with the amount of effort and funds expended by a law firm, can be remarkable. Since personal injury attorneys don't charge initial fees, and instead take a percentage of the settlement or award, an attorney's profit is limited only by their negotiation ability, their litigation skills, or what the court or jury decide is fair remuneration for their clients' injuries. In other words, the only thing limiting how much an attorney can earn, other than the claimant's actual damages, is the ability to effectively advocate. This is partly why I got involved in practicing personal injury law in the first place. Aside from the personal satisfaction derived from offering something positive to an aggrieved client who experienced something terrible, when it came to the litigation process, I was a perfectionist. The idea that I could have so much control over the results was, and continues to be, extremely appealing to me. And I am unaware of any other field of law where you can have as much control over your own destiny and earnings as in personal injury law.

Of course, if something sounds too good to be true, it probably is. There are also some impediments when trying to succeed as a personal injury law firm, especially today. A key motivator to remind yourself of when trying to retain clients is that you're not the only capable law firm in town. Because the ROI for personal injury cases can be so incredibly high, every law firm is competing with hundreds of other law firms for clients. It's not a reason to give up though. It just means that the rulebook for intake from decades ago is no longer acceptable and requires a modern approach to flourish. If you mold your intake department to be successful in today's very competitive personal injury climate, you can quickly leapfrog over competing law firms that are stuck in the past.

There was a time, a decade or two ago, when a personal injury law firm could take a call from a lead, hear the aggrieved circumstances, and ask for a few days' time to review the case before deciding whether or not the attorney wanted to handle the potential client's case (i.e., be retained). I'm sure most of you reading this have experienced or heard of a conversation akin to the following:

> *Claimant*: Hi. I'm looking for an attorney because I was recently injured.
>
> *Attorney*: What happened?
>
> *Claimant*: Well, it's a very convoluted story. [The claimant continues to summarize what happened.]
>
> *Attorney*: Thanks for contacting us. This sounds interesting but today is Friday. What I'd like to do is think about what you just told me over the weekend and give you a call back on Monday to discuss possible next steps.
>
> *Claimant*: Okay. Thank you.

It's very reasonable to believe that some time ago this conversation (despite the lapse of a few days' time) might have nonetheless resulted in a signed client. But, we do not live in this type of world anymore and, if you want to succeed in today's competitive legal environment, you should not operate under the above philosophy.

People today live in a culture, and with an expectation, of instant gratification. All it takes is a smartphone to talk to your friends, order food, or buy groceries—anywhere, anytime, and all in a matter of seconds. This means that people are less and less willing to wait to get what they want, and the ability to view other options is not only feasible but it is literally at their fingertips. If you would search multiple websites to find the cheapest or best hotel room or plane ticket, why wouldn't you do the same when searching for an attorney?

There's only one way to combat this mentality. We must make sure that no matter how many personal injury attorneys the potential client spoke with on the day they contacted your law firm, *they choose you.* You must present a solution that is so appealing that the potential client will be willing to drop everything and sign a contract with your law firm right then and there, without delay. Your intake specialists, or whoever is employed as your first line of communication, should go into every call with one primary focus—if the potential client is qualified for retention, make sure the potential client retains.

Often, people searching for a personal injury attorney would like to shift responsibility of their claim off their shoulders and onto those of an expert as fast as possible. This is understandable—we're talking about those individuals who have often been hurt or wronged, are still reeling from trauma or injury and are likely concerned that they will be taken advantage of by an insurance company, the alleged culpable party or other intermediary. They contacted your law firm in a very vulnerable and often emotional stage in their lives. They don't want a law firm that makes them wait, shifts responsibility back to them (the injured party) to manage their own case, makes them feel like a burden, or, even worse, makes them feel like a number at the grocery store counter. An aggrieved party wants to hire an attorney who makes them feel like they are a priority, they are important to the law firm and they are in good hands. They want a sympathetic presence who will win them with their compassion and interest.

To sign a potential client, nothing is more important than that first phone call. The first impression that your intake department gives is the difference between gaining a new client or one of your competitors gaining a new lead. The best part is that you can *teach* your intake staff how to maximize the results of the very first phone call. Following the guidelines discussed in this book will help you turn new or old leads into signed clients and money spent on marketing campaigns into realized, and substantially increased, revenue.

It's important to be aware of how essential intake is because it's a department and process that is often cloistered off from the rest of the law firm. Intake staff are usually non-attorneys; however, their responsibilities are essential to having a successful and sustainable law practice. Maybe the phones are ringing off the hook, maybe your attorneys are winning every single case that you sign, and maybe you're making more money than you've ever imagined. All of this might be true, and yet your law firm might still be vastly underperforming unbeknownst to you. In other words, sure, the phones are ringing, but how many calls and potential clients are you losing because you have not prioritized your intake process? How many high value cases did you miss out on because your intake was not adequately prepared? The bottom line is this—it's important to stay vigilant and to continue to evaluate your intake processes even if it seems like everything is going right.

Many law firms I've consulted with were initially resistant to the idea that they needed to make changes at the intake level. They brought me in to their law firms with the expectation that I would confirm for them what they already believed to be true—that their intake processes were running efficiently and successfully. I can't tell you how many times I've heard on the first morning of a consult a statement along the following lines: "I have a pretty great intake team and don't expect you to be making any significant changes, but it can't hurt to have you come in and confirm this for me." And my reaction has always been the same, "You're right. It can't hurt." And three days later, at the conclusion of my in-person consulting visit and uncovering significant inefficiencies in the intake process, I would provide an action plan with recommended changes to be implemented within the law firm and, oftentimes, agree to a remote consulting arrangement whereby I would assist with overseeing changes and improvements to the intake department and process going forward. Why? Because once a law firm realizes, through the course of my consulting and identifying trouble areas, how much money may have been lost due to inefficiencies in the intake process, it never wants to repeat such costly errors in the future.

I can tell you right now, that even if you feel like your law firm is doing everything "right", you're still leaving money on the table. I've consulted with law firms nationwide, and I've found massive blind spots in their intake processes every time. Whether it's due to unclear communication between intake specialists and management, not saying the right thing at the right time, hiring specialists unfit for the job, not tracking key performance indicators, not listening to recorded calls or not responding fast enough, I've learned that every intake department and process can benefit from *some* reform.

The important thing to remember here is that struggling law firms are not the only ones that need to regularly reevaluate and possibly reform their intake department and process. Often, it's successful law firms that need their intake addressed the most. Being very successful often leads to less introspection, which means that problems embedded within an intake department and in its processes will fester even more than they would in a struggling law firm that is actively trying to improve. Honesty, self-awareness and accountability are essential if you want to maximize your law firm's potential and increase client retention rates.

The most critical stage of gaining a client is that first phone call that they make to your law firm. In this culture of instant gratification, a good first impression is critical to success. What your intake specialist says on that first phone call has as much to do with whether the potential client retains your law firm as anything else. And the goal is simple on that first phone call: *qualify and become retained.* All the advertising and qualified leads in the world have no monetary import if your intake department cannot convert them into signed clients.

Personal Injury Is A Different Animal

At first glance, it might seem as though personal injury law is a pay-to-play legal field. And let's be honest, on many levels this is almost an accurate assumption. It's an indisputable fact that to succeed in the personal injury world, you must have sufficient funds to market yourself and to hire competent staff. Since the ROI on personal injury cases is significantly higher, there's going to be a lot of well-funded law firms competing with you for the same clients. While this may seem intimidating, it should not dissuade anyone from starting a personal injury law practice. It must be understood and appreciated that you can get outspent and still compete with other law firms, especially if you've overhauled your intake department and process in ways that competing law firms have not considered.

To understand why personal injury law is currently such a competitive industry, let's compare it to the stock market. If I were to tell you I could get you a four- or five-time return from your stock market investment in three to five years, you'd rush to invest your money with me. And I don't blame you. I would be lauded as a miracle worker.

This isn't the same with personal injury cases—what is remarkable is that sometimes your ROI can be even higher than that. Much higher. In my estimation—excluding the homerun cases that most law firms resolve on a yearly basis—the average ROI for a personal injury case is between 10 and 20 times the initial cost per acquisition. And when you compare the cost of advertising to what you can earn on a successful case, it's a no-brainer. Also, consider cases in which your clients were referred to you by a family member or friend. The ROI is literally impossible to calculate—because you didn't spend a penny to generate that lead. And the best part is that if you impress enough people, you won't necessarily have to increase your marketing budget. You will begin to gain a reputation that will automatically generate valuable leads for your law firm. This is what makes personal injury a different animal than any other industries or fields of law—there is a direct relationship between your marketing and your potential ROI.

Most personal injury cases are straightforward and share traits that make litigating them formulaic. Most of the people calling your law firm will be those affected by what we might call negligence cases, such as car accidents, slip and falls, dangerous medications, defective medical devices, medical malpractice, product liability, and so forth. For the majority of negligence cases, you need three things to have a viable claim: (i) clear liability where someone else is at fault; (ii) a resulting injury to your claimant; and (iii) a party responsible with sufficient funds available to resolve claims. It's fairly easy to establish whether your client is injured and whether their case is worthy of retention and investigation. The proving of fault could be a little more time consuming. And, while it may take a few years for these types of cases to resolve, securing negligence cases will put you in an excellent position to recoup your initial investment and much more. (On a personal note: The return associated with personal injury cases isn't just about getting a great ROI for attorneys. The best part about this field is that we are assisting people who need help and have been aggrieved due to the fault of others.)

Another attribute that separates personal injury from other industries or fields of law is that personal injury attorneys work on a contingency fee basis. In other words, we don't charge clients unless and until we win their case and secure a financial settlement or award on their behalf. Now, at first glance, securing 33 to 40 percent of a settlement or award that approaches six or seven figures is a mouth-watering prospect, but this reasonable commission may not seem so reasonable to a given claimant. A layperson does not understand how complicated, time-consuming and expensive litigation can be, and claimants will be very protective of a settlement or award they perceive to be entirely their own. If, at the outset, a claimant does not have context as to why a law firm is asking for one-third or more of the hopeful settlement or award, the potential client might search for a better "deal" elsewhere, or even attempt to represent himself in court to ensure that he receives 100 percent of the potential settlement or award value. To get around this potential issue, it's crucial that intake specialists frame your law firm's legal services in the appropriate way.

Even though a 33 to 40 percent fee may seem high to someone who has just been injured or otherwise aggrieved and has no experience with navigating the personal injury field, the services personal injury attorneys provide should make it well worth the law firm's contingency fee. A good personal injury law firm will, first and foremost, ensure that the litigation process is as seamless as possible for the client throughout the life of the case. This means offering contracts to sign as soon as possible, visiting clients, advocating on their behalf to their adversaries, making the appropriate motions, representing them in court, making themselves available for calls, providing personal and professional advice and ensuring that the client does not get taken advantage of by any opposing parties, all without the clients having to raise a finger. People who have just been through a traumatic incident don't want to spend months trying to navigate the judicial system seeking justice for themselves, and personal injury law firms should make sure the client doesn't have to. If your intake specialist is clear from the start that your law firm will take care of all aspects of the legal process, including securing records, initiating an action, investigating the claims, working to hold others accountable, and seeking to maximize a recovery, it will make the attorney's fee more tenable to the potential client. Your intake specialist should aim to communicate that the law firm will do everything in its power to make the potential client's life easier from the moment they first pick up the phone.

Statistics show that a claimant could acquire three and a half times more money when represented by an attorney than going *pro se*. And the reason for that is that most claimants do not have the necessary resources, experience, or knowledge to manage a case by themselves, which would typically result in a more limited recovery, if any at all. It's essential that law firms make potential clients aware of this at the outset. A potential client also might not be aware of the time it takes to litigate a personal injury case, which can last into the years. These figures alone make hiring a personal injury attorney well worth it, and that's not even considering the peace of mind that comes with having an established, skilled attorney managing the potential client's case. This is the type of information that your intake specialist needs not only to comprehend, but to communicate to potential clients.

Let's not forget that the personal injury attorney fee is contingent. Regardless of how much time, money, effort, or resources a law firm dedicated to a case, personal injury attorneys only get paid if they're successful. Imagine if other industries worked this way: *that is, if a doctor only charged the patients they were able to cure, or a mechanic only charged for the vehicles that they were able to fix*—those would be the only doctors or mechanics in business today. When we agree to represent a claimant, we take our destiny into our own hands and only get paid if we are successful in procuring a settlement or award. If your intake specialist communicates this fact to potential clients concerned by your fee arrangement, it will appear much more reasonable and make them that much more likely to sign with your law firm. Everything I've discussed thus far may seem straightforward, so now let's get to the hard part.

Because personal injury law is such a lucrative field, it's no surprise that more and more people are trying to get involved. Given that the field today is more competitive than ever before, it's essential to distinguish your law firm from the competition. And as stated earlier, since we live in a culture of instant gratification, it's important to realize that any potential client calling your law firm is likely considering other options as well. As a result, your intake specialist should aim to sign potential clients on the very first phone call.

Once the potential client retains your law firm, the intake specialist function is completed, and the intake specialist can proceed to focus on signing the next potential client that calls in. This is why the ability to sign a potential client immediately is so important—it could take your intake specialist 10 to 20 minutes to secure what could become a massive payout for your law firm, after which that same intake specialist will jump right back on the phone lines to secure yet another potential massive payout.

Make no mistake—your intake specialists should be aiming to sign every qualified lead that calls in. The problem for many law firms is that they use the "*except*" scenario to confuse and scare their intake specialists. For example, they may say that the criteria for qualifying and signing are 1-5, but there are five exceptions. And five can quickly become 10. The result? Intake specialists are unable to distinguish what is worthy of seeking retention and what deserves to be rejected. An important takeaway from this book should be: *The simpler the qualification criteria, the easier it will be for your intake specialists to qualify a case on the phone and the more signed retainers you will receive.*

For a law firm to succeed, it must cast as wide a net as possible. Some law firms balk at this—they don't want to sign leads that end up being unqualified or commit to cases they don't have an interest in handling. But in my many years of experience in the personal injury field, there's one thing that I can say for certain—signing a bunch of cases and then dealing with some that might not fit your law firm criteria is far better than the alternative.

Remember: It's better to retain then reject, rather than to reject then regret.

In this extremely competitive legal environment, with a client pool that's more impatient than ever, personal injury attorneys cannot afford to be over selective. There are ways to mitigate signing clients that are not qualified by your law firm's criteria. For example, you can include language in your retainer agreement that protects you in the event of a change of mind, or you can refer cases to other law firms that would like the opportunity to handle the matter. But there is no way to mitigate against turning away potential clients because your qualification criteria is too complicated or selective.

Getting Over The Hump: Realizing Your Law Firm Needs Help

I ask quite a lot from law firms that are interested in my consulting services. If a law firm hires me for a consultation, it is with the expectation that I will get answers to the tough questions—those questions that most attorneys don't want to ask, let alone answer. My consulting services require internal access to intake processes, staff, and law firm metrics, among other things—all with the understanding that my in-depth, results-oriented assessment will lead to significant improvements in intake and ultimately increase a law firm's ROI.

The biggest challenge, however, hasn't been during the actual consulting engagement; rather, it occurs beforehand, when speaking with law firms about a possible consultation. In my experience, law firms have been addicted to the same old processes (especially when they're already profitable). And why go through the trouble of retraining intake specialists, altering attorney responsibilities, and spending more time and effort focusing on intake when you could just continue doing what's been seeming to work for so long? I like to think of this mentality as an addiction. It's not an addiction to success. *It's an addiction to the status quo.* And just like with any other addictions, acceptance is the first step towards making any type of change. If you don't believe you need to change any of your intake processes because they already seem to be operating effectively, now is the time to confirm that belief. If you've been delaying taking a long, hard look at your intake department and process for whatever reason, use this book as the catapult to greater success. If you haven't considered how much more competitive the market has become, now is the time to reconsider. This change in mindset is the hump you need to get over to achieve the maximum number of signed clients and significantly increase your law firm's ROI.

This recommended change in mindset might seem presumptuous, but I can tell you after working with hundreds of law firms nationwide, and listening to thousands of recorded intake calls, I'm convinced that intake problems are pervasive throughout personal injury law firms. Every single law firm I've consulted with has had room for improvement in their intake department and process, and most times that improvement has been dramatic. If you've already conducted a thorough review of your law firm's intake with the goal of improving metrics like conversion percentage and referral profits, you've probably come to the same conclusion and already made drastic changes.

I've always hated the idea of lost opportunities, and I've always aimed for perfection in every endeavor I pursued. I'm certain most attorneys feel the same way. There's not much room for error when litigating cases, as it can have a significant bearing on the outcome. And if you want to be a successful litigator, you must employ a perfectionist's mentality. Yet, many attorneys get so enthralled in perfecting their litigation skills and strategies that they lose sight of the important role intake plays in the success of the law firm. Having a talented and successful team of attorneys means nothing if the attorneys working for you don't have a maximum number of qualified cases to litigate.

Here are some of the questions you can ask yourself as you consider whether your intake department and process have room for improvement:

Are you keeping track of your conversion percentage? If so, how regularly? On a daily basis? Weekly? Monthly?

- Are you reviewing your lost leads?
- Are you listening to your intake specialists on the phone?
- Are you keeping track of your response time on inbound calls? On web leads?
- Are you holding your intake specialists accountable?
- Are you utilizing simple qualification criteria?
- Are you signing cases on the first call?
- Are you employing a "Refer-Before-Reject" model?
- Are you constantly communicating with referral attorneys?
- Are you reviewing the results of your marketing campaigns?
- Are you making attorneys available for intake calls?
- Are you following up with leads appropriately?

If the answer to even just one of the above questions is "no", then you should begin to reevaluate your intake department and process. The sooner you prioritize intake and begin fixing any perceived or actual problems associated with intake, the sooner you will be able to distinguish yourself from competing law firms that refuse to discuss their issues and get over their hump.

I wouldn't be encouraging you to reevaluate your intake department and process if I didn't have years of experience seeing my own methodologies work in every situation I applied them. I've lived and breathed intake for the majority of my professional career—and I know what it takes to succeed in this context. Not every law firm sees the things I see, and many won't even think about intake reform. Such law firms will be the ones you're competing with and I understand how easily one can become complacent when faced with this reality. But at some point, change happens. Either your law firm will get better at intake—or your competitors will.

As an industry, we will get to a point (if not already) where just having a personal injury law firm and marketing presence isn't good enough, and some law firms will go out of business as they cease to remain financially viable. I'm sure that there are some law firms out there that are currently starting to feel the pain of being squeezed by a saturating legal market. For instance, type "car accident attorney" in the search box on Google. How many pages of attorneys are marketing for these types of clients? As personal injury law grows more and more competitive, the number of law firms competing for potential clients' eyes and ears is only getting larger. I implore you to ask yourself these questions:

> *What is it about my law firm that will keep it afloat when the market gets saturated? If my law firm is doing well now, how will it adjust if/when competing law firms begin to re-evaluate their intake department and process, and start to effectively sign potential clients (i.e., take claimants off the market) before they even consider contacting my law firm?*

In general, the legal market won't afford you the time to correct any problems embedded within your law firm's intake. A well-run intake department and process will employ staff well-versed in answering frequently asked questions, knowing qualification criteria, extending empathy, exerting confidence, and providing reassurance. Intake specialists are supposed to anticipate the questions a potential client is going to ask before the questions are posed. They will also try to sign a potential client as soon as possible, getting the potential client out of the extremely competitive legal market before a competing law firm gets the chance to speak with them.

Personal injury law will only get more competitive with time, and there will always be competing law firms, some with greater financial capacity to spend. How you approach this new reality can make the difference regarding your law firm's durability. If you get smart now and make sure to build an intake department and process that works quickly and effectively, you can carve a spot in the legal market for your law firm that law firms refusing to get over their hump will struggle to compete with.

Identifying Key Issues At Intake

I've hopefully established that personal injury law is different from any other field of law; that intake specialists are critical for signing clients; almost every law firm has some type of issue(s) embedded in their intake department and process; and in our culture of instant gratification, claimants will be impatient and will seek out multiple law firms until someone gives them what they're looking for. But how do we prepare, react and adapt to these realities? How do we identify what types of key issues may be harboring in our law firm's intake department and process?

Staffing At All Hours

To begin with, you may have intake specialists working from 9:00 am to 5:00 pm during the week, but who's managing the phones outside of those hours and over the weekend? I've had attorneys look at me like I'm crazy when I asked whether they employ night and/or weekend staff. Their look says, *Why would we need a 24/7 intake department? Can't I let potential clients leave a message? Surely, we can call potential clients back the next business day and sign them. Surely this industry isn't so competitive that I need to have intake specialists on call at every hour of every day.* It's this mentality that causes lost opportunities for so many "weekday hour" law firms.

Think about it: if a potential client calls your law firm and talks to an answering machine or an answering service and then calls another law firm that has a person who can answer questions in real time, qualify the claim, and potentially become retained (all on that first phone call), the potential client is almost certainly not going to wait for your law firm to return their call before choosing the other law firm. By having a person who is available to talk to potential clients at odd hours, a law firm is demonstrating that it has significant resources, cares more than many other law firms, and understands the mentality of someone who has been recently aggrieved and is seeking legal assistance. This is immensely valuable when dealing with personal injury victims.

Using an example, imagine the potential client who was injured in a car accident and broke both of their legs. The potential client is dealing with hospital bills, a present inability to work, is trying to focus on recovery and avoid exacerbating injuries or inadvertently creating new ones, is worried about the burdens placed on loved ones and—for many—the stress of not being able to provide for one's family. Jumping through hoops and dealing with law firm bureaucracy is the last thing that potential client wants to handle. If the potential client calls your law firm and hears an answering machine, do you *really* think they'll have a good first impression of your law firm? Do you *really* think that they'll just sit back idly and wait for your return phone call the next (business) day, as opposed to seeking out another law firm's assistance?

The clients that we represent are often going through a very stressful period in their lives. They're injured, maybe short on cash, and want a solution to their problems as soon as possible. If the potential client starts researching personal injury law firms to assist them, they're often not looking with a discerning eye. Rather, they're looking with an impatient and/or desperate eye. They're stressed, tired, and looking for an attorney who can help immediately. Put yourself in their shoes. If you're reaching out for help, and the first nine law firms you contact send you to an answering machine, but the tenth law firm has a live representative who knows what questions to ask and has answers to your questions, which law firm are you going to be most impressed by? Which law firm are you most likely going to entrust with your legal matter? If your intake specialists can speak with potential clients overnight or on the weekends, they can potentially sign the potential client fairly instantly, taking the potential client off the market before less ambitious law firms have the opportunity to even listen to their voicemails. While you sleep, your intake staff could be signing clients and increasing potential revenue for your law firm, either through your own eventual earned attorney's fees or through referral fees.

So, remember this: *at the intake stage, a personal injury law firm doesn't have the luxury to delay anything!* This realization is the first step towards reforming your intake department and process and maximizing your law firm's ROI, but it's far from the last. You can have the right mindset, but that means nothing if you can't execute correctly.

Providing Training And Decision-Making Authority

Let's next assume that you have an intake staff (in-house or outsourced) working 24 hours a day, seven days a week. You must empower those intake specialists to make certain decisions so that you ensure maximized returns for their efforts. You can do this by giving them clear guidelines as to what you're trying to accomplish, what types of cases they should be qualifying, and how to make your law firm so appealing that the potential client is interested in immediately retaining your law firm. The concept bears repeating: *to put yourself at the front of the law firm pack, your intake specialists must have certain decision-making authority—meaning the power to qualify cases and sign potential clients while on the very first phone call.*

I recognize that to have this decision-making authority takes a lot of training, trust, and initiative. The intake specialist picking up the phone must be versed enough in the legal process and case types to know whether the potential client has a qualifying claim that would likely net a return for your law firm. You can have a great, amicable, friendly intake staff, but if they don't have the means to qualify a claim and sign a potential client by the end of that first phone call, that's a potential client who will likely continue seeking out other law firms for assistance.

If that potential client hangs up the phone with your intake specialist and calls another law firm that has given its intake specialists the tools to qualify a claim and the decision-making authority to sign, that potential client can retain the other law firm almost immediately, taking the potential client off the market. In that instance, all the effort your intake specialist invested on the phone call and, if applicable, the marketing dollars you spent, would have yielded zero return. You shouldn't put your law firm at such a huge disadvantage when compared to competing law firms by not empowering your intake specialists to make certain decisions and sign qualified claimants.

Another tidbit: *strike while the iron is hot.* A potential client is generally the most interested in your law firm on that first phone call with your intake specialist. The internet gives those of us in personal injury significant advantages by offering a potential client the ability to sign a retention agreement digitally (over the internet). If your law firm isn't taking advantage of a service like this, I strongly encourage your law firm to consider doing so.

A lack of decision making authority on the part of your intake specialist or offering to call the potential client back with a final decision on whether you will handle their claim(s), can be a death knell to your chances to sign that potential client. If your intake specialists are not able to qualify and/or sign a potential client as soon as possible, the potential client will likely lose interest or retain another law firm. This happens to law firms every single day and to mitigate the frequency of it happening to your law firm, you need a dedicated intake department with the knowledge, experience, decision making authority and ability to communicate with potential clients in a way that makes them eager to retain your legal services. But please don't confuse this concept with being selfish. Part of an intake department's success depends on the ability of its intake specialists to be *selfless.*

Ability To Listen And Empathize

When I suggest that intake specialists can be selfish, I mean that intake specialists tend to talk much more about their law firm than spend adequate time speaking about the potential client. I'm endlessly frustrated when I listen to a recorded intake call, and the first question the intake specialist asks is: "How did you hear about us?"

Really?!

The first phone call should not begin with a focus on the law firm. It should begin with a focus on the potential client and the reason(s) the potential client is looking for legal assistance. If you're a potential client who's calling law firms looking for support after being injured or otherwise aggrieved, the last thing you want to do is massage the law firm's ego and answer questions about how you came upon the law firm's advertisements.

> *The small benefit of knowing how the potential client heard about your law firm gives the law firm insight into advertising analytics, but it is far outweighed by how self-centered that question may appear to a potential client. Moreover, it's a detail that can be learned, if necessary, at a later point after the potential client has been retained.*

Remember, the potential client didn't contact your law firm to fill out a marketing survey—they contacted your law firm because they want a solution(s) to their problem(s). They want someone to provide answers and, most importantly, offer reassurance and guidance. The only questions we should be asking the potential client on that initial phone call are questions about the caller's circumstances.

Another tremendous concern I've had after listening to hundreds of recorded intake calls is the general *lack of empathy*. Okay, I get it. Intake specialists need to be attentive and engaged on every phone call. This is not an easy task. Have you ever tried being polite, respectful, and interested on every phone call you received? It's nearly impossible. We get distracted, annoyed and, sometimes, must deal with very unpleasant people. However, regardless of how difficult this may seem, there is no room for intake specialists who are impersonal and clinical with a potential client, neglecting to explore questions about the potential client's circumstances and/or informing them about how the legal process generally works. When an intake specialist is asking a potential client about their accident, the intake specialist must look for opportunities to be empathetic, reassuring and/or appropriately responsive as to the potential client's misfortune. If, instead, an intake specialist is robotically asking questions about what the potential client's injury is, where the injury happened, and who may be responsible, the potential client isn't going to feel reassured in any way. In fact, they'll likely be distressed by having to relive their past traumas. Addressing this can be as simple as saying:

> "I'm so sorry this happened to you."
>
> "We're on your side and will work hard to make sure that the responsible parties are held accountable and work to get you compensation for your injuries."
>
> "We know what we're doing, and we'll make sure that the legal process will be as easy as possible for you."

Making a potential client feel like you're there for them will go a long way toward building a relationship of trust that will ultimately lead to a retained case.

So, the question becomes "why?" Why do we make this about us? Why are we so robotic when speaking with potential clients? Why are we only hiring intake specialists to work from 9:00 am to 5:00 pm, Monday through Friday? Why are we not putting the potential client first? In two words: entitlement *and* contentment. We cannot take leads for granted. We cannot assume that because a potential client contacted our law firm, they already decided to retain our legal services. This assumption undoubtedly leads to many lost opportunities. An attorney I worked with some years ago referred to this as the "fat cat syndrome," which signifies the concept that law firms get lazy when they're successful (even though their intake department and process may be underperforming). They're making money, so why should the law firm look to reform intake? From the surface, this would seem like a plausible argument, and that the effort expended to improve intake would be an unnecessary use of time and money. But there are many flaws with this mindset.

The first and most obvious flaw—using the fat cat syndrome analogy again—is that the fatter the cat gets, the less active it becomes. In other words, the more content you are with your law practice, the fewer improvements you look to make and the less agile your law firm becomes in a constantly evolving, competitive legal market. There are law firms that have been enlightened by having an empathetic intake department with the offer of immediate service/retention, and those that have done so are growing and signing clients at a far superior rate. Law firms that stay complacent and don't look to exude empathy for potential clients are going to shrink, and the fat cats will realize that the mice are a little faster than they used to be.

You can't afford to make this realization too late. At the end of the day, as I mentioned before, personal injury law is a business as much as it is a profession, and business is ruthless. The legal market won't forgive you for failing to accommodate a potential client's needs, and neither will potential clients. With a field as crowded and competitive as personal injury law, even the most established law firms cannot afford to remain content. If fear doesn't motivate you, what should motivate you is the potential increase in revenue that your law firm never realizes by not being more proactive with your intake department and process. In my consultations with law firms, I've watched law firm retention rates increase by up to 40 percent by implementing my recommendations—making simple changes—in the intake process.

Providing Great Customer Service

When it comes to customer service, which is what intake essentially is, a reassuring voice is a positive attribute that can help your law firm retain more clients. In my personal life, I've experienced how valuable a calm and reassuring customer service voice can be during a stressful time. About two years ago I had some technical issues with my cellphone. I asked colleagues and friends, and did extensive research on the internet, but nothing seemed to help fix my issues. I estimated that I spent more than 20 hours over the phone with various support technicians over a three-month period troubleshooting. I was incredibly frustrated each time I contacted customer support, but what the technician told me on each call calmed me down: "Okay, we've seen that before. We're going to get this fixed for you." You can imagine how upset I was, especially by hour 19 when my cellphone was not yet fixed, but how the technicians addressed me on each call helped put my concerns at ease and elicited a feeling of trust between them and me.

The moral to my cellphone saga is that when a potential client who has been injured or otherwise aggrieved contacts your law firm for assistance, it is crucial to reassure them that they made the right decision by contacting your law firm and that they are in good hands. Your intake specialists should communicate that your law firm has plenty of experience, especially (if applicable) in handling claims similar to the potential client's, and that the law firm is willing, able, and interested in handling the potential client's case. Making the potential client feel like they made the right decision by contacting your law firm increases the chance that you're going to be the last law firm they call.

Communicating A Sense Of Immediacy

Balancing empathy for potential clients and good customer service with a desire to increase your law firm's retention rate/revenue may seem like a challenging task, but I've found in my years of intake experience a strategy that works a majority of the time. Your intake specialists should communicate to potential clients that your law firm wants to begin working with/for them as soon as possible. To do this, your intake specialist's conversation must be punctuated with a sense of interest and urgency throughout. Hundreds of intake calls I've listened to have ended with the intake specialist scheduling (or not scheduling) an in-person sign-up and then concluding the call. The intake specialist rarely assured the potential client that his claim is exactly the type of claim the law firm can assist with (and, if applicable, regularly handles) and, perhaps more importantly, never tells the potential client that the law firm would like to start the investigation process on their behalf immediately. There shouldn't be any hesitation around signing a potential client to a retainer—that's what you want to do, and that's what the potential client is hoping for. Keep in mind, they called your law firm seeking legal assistance and representation.

Immediately is one of those magic words I've found to be very effective in increasing a law firm's conversion percentage (more on this metric later). It is crucial to emphasize to potential clients that not only are you interested in handling their case, but that you also want to get working on their behalf right away. If intake specialists integrate a sense of immediacy into their conversations with potential clients, it will do wonders for your conversion percentage numbers.

Providing Decision-Making Authority—Revisited

I spoke about this earlier, but it's worthy of visiting again. Some law firms are reluctant to give their intake specialists the authority to make qualification decisions in order to sign cases, without first speaking with an attorney. Some of the reasons I've heard for this reluctance are as follows:

> What if the intake specialist acquires a signed retainer for a case that's not qualified?
>
> What if the intake specialist acquires a signed retainer for a case that won't have the ROI I want, or isn't in my area of expertise?
>
> What if the intake specialist acquires a signed retainer for a case that I must subsequently reject?

I've been focusing on intake for years, and I've found that the concerns articulated above are never as severe as attorneys deem them to be. They're real and legitimate concerns, but there are simple ways to resolve them. Besides, if you're truly prioritizing intake, these concerns should rarely (if at all) become real concerns for you. Let's go through different scenarios.

> *Scenario One—Your intake specialist acquires a signed retainer for a case that's not qualified.*

The first thing you worry about is a waste of effort and funds associated with the sign-up process. But let's be honest. Isn't this just a cost of doing business? If you're running a law firm and you only expect to sign cases that are *certain* to have value, you're cutting yourself short and significantly limiting your law firm's ROI. Think about how many cases you've signed that you initially thought were small value cases that, after investigation and work-up, became some of your largest sources of revenue.

It happens in almost every single law firm! And for this reason, it is beneficial to err on the side of signing and accepting that mistakes may happen—or that post-retention rejection determinations may need to be made. However, to maximize revenue, it's certainly reasonable to anticipate that your intake specialists might acquire a signed retainer from a client who doesn't have a qualified claim. In those scenarios, the process you have in place to realize this mistake and reject an unqualified claim becomes exceedingly important. For example, I would strongly recommend incorporating in your intake process that all newly signed cases are immediately reviewed by an attorney to determine whether to pursue or reject early on.

Scenario Two—Your intake specialist acquires a signed retainer with a statute of limitations that is fast approaching, and you don't think it's worth pursuing. Now you're stuck.

Not so fast. Understand that *being retained* does not, and should not, mean that your law firm is certain to resolve the case for a potential client. What being retained should mean for any personal injury law firm is that you were given the opportunity to begin an investigation of the claims on behalf of the client. There are plenty of times where a potential client tells you something at the outset and, as you undertake your investigation, you learn that something different or contrary has occurred. In that case, a court of law couldn't reasonably expect you to continue to represent the client. Here's some advice: Review your retention agreements to confirm it has specific language stating that *being retained gives the law firm permission to begin an investigation on behalf of the client and, should the law firm decide not to proceed with the matter, the law firm could cease representation.* While this is not guaranteed to protect you, it certainly helps.

(Some more advice and as a side note: Stop using unreasonably long retainer agreements. The longer the retention agreement, the less likely the potential client will read it, and the less likely the potential client will sign it.)

Scenario Three—Your law firm doesn't have the expertise to handle the type of case signed by your intake specialist. Now you're stuck with a case and you have no idea how to proceed.

One of the best aspects about our profession is our ability to work together and refer cases to each other based on experience, subject matter expertise and/or resources, to name a few. And, quite often, that referral arrangement will yield a referral fee for your law firm. I'm not going to get into each state's rules on referral fees other than to say that it would behoove you to actively consider whether you can refer cases in return for a referral fee, based on state law.

Let's rewind for a moment. The best way to "fix" mistakes is to make sure they don't happen in the future. To do this, you must have a system in place to help you discover wrong choices before they lead to a waste of resources. However, if a wrong decision to qualify and/or sign a potential client is discovered—whether prior to the retention or post-retention—you should use it as a teaching opportunity for your intake department each time. Explain what the mistake was, why it happened and how it could be avoided in the future. The result? Your intake specialists will become more experienced and gain a better understanding of their responsibilities, and you will only lose a few minutes out of your day.

I know, I know. Who has this time to go over mistakes though, right? Well, if you're looking to maximize your retention opportunities and, ultimately, ROI, I promise you this time will be well spent.

Loosening The Qualification Criteria

I firmly believe that, in the personal injury law field, if you want to maximize revenue, you need to loosen your signing or qualification criteria. Something that really bothers me is the narrow-minded sentiment expressed by some law firms that they *only want to sign high value cases.* Why? As indicated earlier, law firm margins can be so favorable that it is in your best interest to sign all cases that *may* have value (whether high or low). Too often, I see law firms using the below criteria at intake:

> *We only qualify cases that are certain to be valuable.*

This standard is not only too strict, but it is flawed. How do you know what is *certain* to be valuable at the intake phase? Potential clients are often mistaken about their injuries and events that it is virtually impossible to label a case as certain to be *anything.* And if it's virtually impossible to assess the actual value attributed to a claim at the intake phase, how many cases do you think a law firm using such strict criteria is losing each year under such a standard?

Want to increase revenue? Loosen your qualification criteria. Give the potential client the benefit of the doubt. Give your intake specialists the ability to allow your legal team to turn what was thought to be a small value case into a higher value one. Take advantage of your referral relationships. And, most importantly, begin to use appropriate qualification criteria. What qualification criteria should you use?

Begin to qualify cases based upon whether they could be valuable.

At the end of the day, it's much better to retain cases with the understanding that some might not prove to be valuable than it is to miss out on cases by not having a sufficiently broadened mentality. You'll make much more money with the "could be" strategy than you will with the "certain to be" strategy.

The Intake Bridge: Convincing Qualified Claimants To Sign With You!

By this point, I hope I've persuaded you of the need to take a long, hard look at your intake department and process (and to regularly do so) for the sake of longevity and continued success of your law firm in an extremely competitive legal market. So now that you've been persuaded about the importance of intake and want to get to work, where do you begin?

The first and most important touchpoint in intake occurs on that first phone call from a potential client, during which your intake specialist should be looking to have the claimant signed. In order to convince the potential client to sign with your law firm, your intake specialist must position your law firm in the most appealing light possible. I call this critical touchpoint *the intake bridge*—the point where the potential client is deciding whether they want to cross your law firm's bridge by signing a retention agreement, thereby placing their legal matter in your capable hands. *A high-functioning intake department will not only make the other side of that bridge look great, but it will also make crossing the bridge seem almost effortless for the potential client.*

Putting a lot of work into building, maintaining, and selling your law firm bridge is so important because—as I've stated before—you're not the only bridge in town. The potential client contacting your law firm will likely be considering other paths too and might have already decided against bridges that weren't welcoming or easy enough to cross. It's your intake department's responsibility to make them cross your law firm bridge right then and there, to get them over to your law firm as a retained client.

The winning bridge is the one that asks the potential client to do the least and expect the most.

I've discussed the concept of anticipating your competition before, but I have yet to use one of my favorite analogies. I call it the *blackjack mentality*. It's simple to understand, especially if you've gambled before, and if you have your own law firm and invested time and money into marketing your legal services to the public with the hopes that qualified claimants would contact your law firm and sign with you, then you, my friend, have gambled. But back to my analogy.

When you play blackjack, you're playing against the house, not the other players, and the goal is always to beat the dealer. The dealer plays with one card face down, and the blackjack player must guess whether their combination of cards is strong enough to beat the dealer's hand. An experienced blackjack player will assume that the dealer's face down card has a value of ten and centers their betting strategy around that assumption. Experienced players utilize this strategy because it maximizes their odds of winning any given hand, while also keeping them from getting too comfortable and inadvertently deviating from the ultimate goal—to beat the dealer.

At intake, law firms must make a similar assumption which will maximize their odds of signing clients. Your blackjack mentality is that no matter how wonderful a potential client sounds, no matter how interested they seem in your legal services, or whether they've retained your law firm in the past, you *must assume the potential client spoke with a law firm before contacting yours and is prepared to contact another law firm afterwards.* With this mentality, you won't allow yourself to grow complacent. More pointedly, law firms shouldn't expect that the potential client will get around to signing a retainer that was sent over email (or overnight mail), or that the potential client will come into your law firm if you scheduled an in-person sign-up for the next day. No matter how enthusiastic the potential client seems, you must act as if they're going to look at other law firm options during the time they remain on the market.

Of course, in an ideal world, this won't happen, and they'll sign a retainer with your law firm while on the phone with your intake specialist. But how do you get to that point? How do you get to the point of convincing a potential client to cross your law firm bridge—and no one else's—as fast as possible? Simply put, with preparation and hard work.

Let's delve further into the literal, physical world of bridges to discuss how to accomplish this. If I had to literally cross bridges to get to attorneys, what kind of bridge would I choose? I'd probably lean towards something that makes crossing seem easy—something like a moving walkway. Having to do almost no work to get to the other side of the bridge is something I strongly support and will be appealing to potential clients as well. The more effort that is being asked, the less interested the potential client is likely to be. Intake specialists should guide potential clients towards your law firm every step of the way and ensure that the potential client is not expending too much effort to sign with your law firm. Sure, a moving walkway might be more complicated and expensive to maintain, but traditional bridges are a dime a dozen for claimants. You should make sure that the process of crossing your law firm bridge is so effortless that potential clients won't even consider more traditional bridge options offered by competing law firms.

Never underestimate the power of telling a potential client, "Don't worry about anything. We'll take care of everything from this point forward." Getting them to take those steps onto your moving walkway, where suddenly the potential client isn't exerting any significant effort and is just being guided by your law firm, is all you need to do.

However, it's not just about building a better bridge; it's about selling it! Potential clients will not want to cross your law firm bridge if they're not encouraged by what's on the other side. Potential clients need to believe your law firm can provide the best results possible for them. An intake specialist can help foster this sense of confidence in potential clients by taking control from the moment they pick up the phone. In this regard, it's important that intake specialists do three things on every qualified call:

1. *Convey reassurance that the potential client did the right thing by contacting your law firm.*

2. *Convey an interest in working with/helping the potential client.*

3. *Convey a sense of urgency to proceed with retaining your law firm.*

Don't make the first phone call from a potential client more difficult than it needs to be. Don't ask for police reports, a doctor's statement/hospital report, proof of injury or evidence of insurance, at least not before your law firm is retained. If a potential client is shopping for law firms and one law firm asks for documentation before retention while the other law firm does not, it's easy to guess which law firm is likely to be retained. If your law firm bridge is easier to cross than others and seems to offer exactly what the potential client is looking for (i.e., superior legal representation), most of your work is done.

You can also *wow* potential clients by taking a page out of the playbook of car dealerships. When a car dealership wants to "close a deal" (regardless of how well the salesperson is getting along with the potential buyer, how likely it seems the potential client will purchase a car, or how busy the dealership may be), the salesperson brings in a manager to complete the transaction—*every single time*. Why? Because the manager has a title, which comes with an aura of power that makes the customer feel special. This basic strategy is often what closes the deal for so many car sales, so why don't law firms employ a similar strategy? Why doesn't every single personal injury law firm have an attorney get on the phone with every single qualified lead? Since we're following the blackjack mentality, why wouldn't we want to pull out all the tricks to elevate ourselves above competing law firms that potential clients are also considering?

If a potential client contacts four law firms, it's unlikely that more than one or two of them will put the client on the phone with an attorney. And this is how you can really, and immediately, distinguish yourself from competing law firms, and convince potential clients to cross your law firm bridge first. My philosophy here is to get an attorney involved with every single qualified claimant by putting them on the phone whenever a claimant expresses some doubt or hesitation with moving forward. And, if you don't get a potential client retained on that first phone call, having an attorney call the potential client back is the best way to rekindle their interest in your law firm. Moreover, if the potential client has a legal question that your intake specialist doesn't understand or shouldn't be responding to, the "on-call" attorney is an impressive fallback option. Your attorney is your ace in the hole, the person to ensure that the potential client signs a retainer as soon as possible.

But let's not sell intake specialists short. They are your first line of communication. And when on the phone with potential clients, your intake specialists need to have the right mentality. They need to be positive and friendly, attentive, prepared to answer frequently asked questions, knowledgeable of the subject matter and able to convey a sense of urgency. And just as importantly, they should be operating under the mentality of "sign, then investigate" to get that potential client across your law firm bridge and off the market as soon as possible. And this mentality must be supported by the possibility of having an attorney involved to "close" on the retention.

The Importance Of Persistent Follow-Up

I emphasize the importance of getting potential clients signed on that first phone call because I find it by far to be the best strategy for law firms to ultimately sign clients. However, if your intake specialists are unable to sign a potential client on that first phone call, you shouldn't give up! You should follow-up consistently with potential clients until you are certain that either they aren't interested, have chosen another law firm or have become unresponsive by your law firm's definition. *This bears repeating.* Your law firm should not stop following up with a potential client until either:

1. *The potential client informs you that they are no longer interested in your law firm.*

2. *The potential client informs you that they retained another law firm to assist in the matter.*

3. *The potential client is unresponsive for a significant period of time.*

From my experience, many law firms make a costly assumption when it comes to follow-up endeavors. This assumption is that a potential client must not be interested in their legal services since the potential client hasn't responded to the law firm's multiple phone call attempts. By assuming this, we are making it again about the law firm and not the claimant. What do I mean here? We are not considering all, or many, of the daily distractions that a potential client may have that is preventing them from returning the phone call(s). Think about this for a minute.

For many potential clients, contacting a law firm is just an idea. Many of them don't understand the time constraints associated with starting a lawsuit and often, it's taken the potential client weeks, if not months, to even pick up the phone in the first place despite having been injured or otherwise aggrieved. And here you are assuming that because the potential client hasn't returned your phone call in over a week, it means they're not interested in your legal services. One of the most beneficial changes I recommend when I consult with law firms is to prolong the timeframe for follow-up attempts to unresponsive claimants. Instead of giving up after one week, I ask the law firm to double or even triple that time period. And what I've observed because of this elongated follow-up period is an exponential increase in retention rates for those law firms.

As an aside, in addition to consulting law firms on the intake process, I am also the CEO of an outsourced intake department—Intake Conversion Experts (ICE). At ICE, to maximize retention for law firm clients, we utilize a persistent and prolonged follow-up process that has resulted in great success. Specifically, ICE specialists continue to follow-up with potential clients until the ICE specialist reaches at least one month without client response. Does this mean we call every day? Of course not! However, quite often we'll connect with a potential client after a few weeks of silence and the best part is the potential client will often share with the ICE specialist, unsolicited, the reason for their lack of response, further communicating a sense of appreciation of the follow-up efforts. Does it work every single time? Maybe not. But it works more often than you can imagine. And this is just one way that we can maximize retention for our law firm clients.

What I can tell you unequivocally, is that most law firms give up on their leads way too early in the intake process and that plays a critical role in the lost opportunities for signing clients. Remember the three reasons you should stop following up with a potential client. And if one of those reasons does not exist, persistent follow-up should be employed. There are literally hundreds of reasons a viable and interested claimant may not have crossed your law firm bridge yet. And operating under the assumption that a claimant must not be interested in your legal services due to their lack of contact with your law firm is not only misplaced, it is detrimental to your law firm's success.

The Value Of Intake Metrics

Owning your own personal injury law firm requires a significant investment. To acquire a substantial number of leads, law firms must invest a considerable amount of time and money marketing their legal services. However, to ensure that their expenditures are justified, they must do everything in their power to maximize their marketing ROI. To maximize your law firm's ROI, you must be aware of certain intake metrics that indicate how well (or poorly) your law firm is doing. In this regard, one metric is more important than any other and, in my opinion, must be reviewed, assessed, considered and monitored on a frequent basis to ensure a law firm's ongoing success. What I'm referring to is a law firm's *conversion percentage.* Now, I understand that every industry uses the term conversion percentage differently to make it relevant to the product(s) or service(s) being offered, so what does the *conversion percentage* for law firms mean?

In its simplest form, a law firm's conversion percentage is the percentage of qualified leads that a law firm successfully turns into signed clients/retained cases. For example:

> *If your law firm acquired 100 leads and 50 of them qualified for retention, to determine your law firm's conversion percentage, you would need to know how many of those 50 qualified leads your law firm ultimately signed. If 25 of those qualified leads were signed, your conversion percentage would be 50 percent (25/50).*

This metric is valuable for many reasons, not the least of which is because it separates your law firm's marketing statistics from its intake statistics. The two are often mistakenly conflated—but shouldn't be. If your marketing results are poor, you might not be receiving a lot of calls or leads, or you might be receiving a lot of *unqualified* calls or leads. Even if the volume of qualified leads contacting your office is small, your intake department can still be successful if it is able to sign a significant portion of those qualified leads. Marketing ceases the moment a lead contacts your law firm. Everything from that moment forward becomes the responsibility of your intake department—the connector guiding that qualified lead across your law firm bridge.

A significant blind spot that many law firms have is in the way they record profits. In many businesses, different categories are tracked separately in how they contribute to the profit and loss of the company. Most law firms don't do this. A law firm can earn $20 million in a year and think it's doing great, while not taking a deeper dive into those numbers and exposing what could be significant failings, particularly with intake and its conversion percentages. And the best part is, a law firm can break up this number in a multiple of ways. For instance, law firms should be reviewing their conversion percentages on at least a month-to-month and year-to-year basis for:

- Different types of cases
- Different intake specialists
- Different days of the week
- Different regions
- Different marketing campaigns
- Different marketers
- Different methods of contact

It's shocking to me that many law firms I work with haven't tracked these numbers. Without them, a law firm has no meaningful way of determining whether a specific marketing campaign was effective or whether your intake department is underperforming.

When I talk about effectiveness, I'm referring to some established averages that measure how often law firms can convert certain types of cases. This number varies depending on the type of case being analyzed. For example, for mass tort cases, an average law firm converts between 50 and 60 percent of the qualified leads they want to sign. For general negligence cases, this number is a bit higher, with an average law firm converting between 70 and 80 percent of the qualified leads they want to sign.

Now, these are the numbers for an average law firm that either hasn't scrutinized its intake department and process, considered many of the intake metrics necessary to evaluate its total law firm performance, or asked an intake expert to review its processes. For law firms applying my strategies and adopting my philosophy, I would expect those numbers to be substantially higher. That is, I would expect at least a 75 percent conversion rate for mass tort cases and 90 percent conversion rate for general negligence cases. Why this disparity in conversion percentages for different types of cases? It's simple. The conversion percentages are higher for local cases because you can meet with potential clients in person, often within a few hours of the potential client contacting your law firm. Moreover, potential clients are more familiar with the concept of general negligence than they are with mass torts. When you run national campaigns, which are the norm for mass tort campaigns, that option is not as feasible.

If you're not tracking these numbers and setting concrete goals for your intake department and law firm, you're doing your law firm a disservice. It's easy to stay unaware if your law firm is already successful, but no matter how much money you generate, I would suspect that you're not signing every qualified lead you want. Improvements begin with tracking appropriate statistics, evaluating your weaknesses based on those numbers, and then understanding and prioritizing the improvements necessary to maximize returns.

A crucial mistake that keeps the conversion percentages of many intake departments lower than it should be is in the process of determining whether a potential client qualifies for retention. I've touched on this concept in previous chapters, but it's especially relevant when ensuring your law firm's conversion percentage is as high as possible. To get an accurate assessment of your conversion percentage, your intake specialists must decide whether a lead qualifies for retention or not *on that very first phone call.* The value of the particular case shouldn't be critical at this initial stage—your intake specialists don't need to know whether the case will make a significant return for your law firm or any return for that matter—but a fundamental understanding of what makes a case qualify for retention and investigation is essential.

Put simply, maximizing your law firm's conversion percentage starts with a trust that your intake specialists are well tasked to handle qualification on their own. Of course, this doesn't mean just turning your intake specialists loose and hoping for the best; there should be sufficient (and ongoing) training and a set of guidelines created for your intake specialists that clearly define what qualifies a case for retention and empowers them to sign if a case fits within those guidelines.

I've said this before, but too many law firms have criteria for qualification that's either too stringent or confusing, or the law firm has no criteria at all with the hopes of being able to investigate the potential claim before retention. These policies stifle intake specialists and leave them without the freedom and power to make decisions and assist your law firm in maximizing its ROI. What law firms should be evaluating is whether a case qualifies for *further investigation* or not. If the answer to that question is "yes", then the intake specialist should make signing the potential client their priority. Once you've established clear guidelines for what qualifies a case for retention, you can begin analyzing the strengths or weaknesses of your intake department by looking at what percentage of those qualified cases are ultimately signed.

When a law firm requests my consulting services, one of the first questions I ask is: "How many cases did your law firm sign last month compared to how many cases you wanted to sign?" Far too often, a law firm's response is that it signed all the cases it wanted. Let's discuss a hypothetical that has likely happened, in one form or another, to most law firms to illustrate why this answer is probably not accurate:

> *A potential client contacts your personal injury law firm and says, "I was recently in a car accident. I was injured and was taken to the hospital. I'm not sure whether the person who hit me has insurance. The police arrived but I don't have a copy of the report that they completed. And I'm not sure what my next steps are."*

With phone calls like this, far too many law firms assume they have the luxury of time to wait and investigate the claim prior to deciding to sign the case. Intake specialists ask the potential client to do some research on their own, obtain a copy of the police report, or get a better idea of the applicable insurance policies. The law firm thinks it's made a shrewd decision that will save the law firm time and money. But have they? It seems to me all they've really done is set that potential client free to contact another law firm that perhaps won't be as demanding as they were on the first phone call.

This is bad enough, but many law firms seek to rationalize their actions when this type of scenario leads the demanding law firm to lose the potential client. If the law firm that asked the potential client to do all the groundwork follows-up after that initial phone call, it's likely that the potential client will inform them they ultimately hired another law firm. And if the demanding law firm was tracking intake metrics accurately, it would identify this case as one they wanted to sign but failed to, which would bring their conversion percentage down. What many law firms do instead, however, is not count that case against their conversion percentage. Instead, they will rationalize this lost opportunity by saying the potential client was not a qualified lead to begin with. Almost every single law firm I've worked with has this same issue (to some degree) *of kicking the can down the road* before committing to wanting the case. This way, law firms mistakenly convince themselves that they've signed every case they *really* wanted.

Hypothetical cases, like the one above, should absolutely qualify for investigation (remember—that's the standard), and an effective intake specialist should jump at the chance to sign the potential client who indicated they were injured in a car accident where another vehicle hit their vehicle. In this culture of instant gratification, we no longer have the luxury to investigate a claim before retention. The more honest a law firm is about its conversion percentages and the more freedom you give your intake specialists, the better you can judge how your law firm is performing on this crucial intake metric.

If your law firm commits to addressing its problems with conversion and intake seriously, the rewards can reach far beyond this newfound self-awareness. I've consulted with law firms that had conversion percentages between 40 and 50 percent before I arrived, which skyrocketed up to 80 percent in the first month I spent with them. This doesn't just apply to floundering law firms either; I've worked with many law firms that already had conversion percentages in the mid-80's that grew into the mid-90's after I worked with them. When you hold yourself accountable for that simple decision to qualify or not and strive to make that decision on the first phone call, you can exponentially improve the performance of your law firm and substantially impact its ROI.

Law firms worry that by loosening their criteria for qualifying a case, they'll end up with some unwanted cases. That's a valid concern and probable outcome. Some of the cases your law firm signs for investigation will certainly be unqualified. They won't be able to make you money, or the claimant will be exaggerating about their injury or right to reimbursement. But here's a novel question: *What's wrong with signing an unqualified case?*

There's an old fishing analogy which you've probably heard a thousand times before that fits perfectly here. When you're fishing, the best way to catch the most fish possible is by casting a wide net. Sure, casting a wide net will capture some unwanted fish (and even some garbage) and you'll end up throwing those fish back into the water. But there's no more effective way to catch the most fish that you *do* want to keep than by casting a wide net. Of course, there is an alternative. You can spend a tremendous amount of time trying to create the best system to catch the biggest fish that you want. Be forewarned though. This will undoubtedly result in hundreds, if not thousands, of really appealing fish getting away.

A great thing about casting a wide net is that you don't have to keep the unwanted fish. The same generally applies to unqualified leads that are signed. I tell every law firm I consult with to draft their retention agreements in a way that potential clients acknowledge the following: (i) they are hiring a law firm with the understanding that the retainer gives the law firm permission to begin an investigation on the client's behalf, and (ii) should the law firm determine that it is uninterested in representing the claimant for any reason, the law firm may disengage the client at that time. However, some law firms that have protective language, like the above, in their retainer agreements are still reluctant to sign potential clients. The rationale being that they don't want to waste valuable resources on a lead that won't end up procuring an attorney's fee. This sounds reasonable on the surface, but it's yet another example of law firms being satisfied with the *status quo* and not truly looking to maximize their ROI.

When applying this "cast a wider net" practice, there will certainly be some cases that don't go anywhere. There will be some cases to which you devote resources to verify police reports, track down medical records, and demand the insurance information of the person who injured your client, and you end up discovering that you can't make money on the case and may, in fact, have lost some money in time and resources spent. This *will* happen, and it will be very frustrating when it does. But given the margins available in personal injury law, it's foolish to let examples like these dissuade you from signing as many potentially viable cases as possible. For every case that results in a dead end, there will be many more cases that end up netting your law firm a substantial return. You must be willing to accept some failures if you want your law firm to sustain great success.

This is why I really don't buy the "if it ain't broke, don't fix it" mentality many law firms adopt when it comes to intake. My experience has uncovered an ugly truth—that many law firms are getting by despite having poor intake processes. And when you're already spending so much money to get potential clients to contact your law firm, why not spend a few additional resources (in the way of time and training, above all) to make sure that qualified leads don't become lost opportunities?

The brave new world of personal injury law requires law firms to be conscious of, and engage in, more methods of communication with potential clients than ever before. Nowadays, most marketing law firms don't just focus on getting potential clients to contact your law firm by phone. They also try engaging potential clients over the internet, whether through social media or search engine optimization. When dealing with internet-based communication, we must invoke the blackjack mentality again, maybe even more aggressively than over the phone. Because of the extremely passive nature of the internet, potential clients contacting your law firm over the internet are likely considering and engaging with other law firms at the very same time they're communicating with yours and in the very same manner. This means that the first law firm to respond puts itself in the best position to sign that potential client.

But responding isn't enough. *Remember: You must be able to qualify the lead immediately and, if qualified, give the potential client an instant mechanism for signing your law firm's retention agreement.* When communicating with potential clients over the internet, response time is by far the most important intake metric to track whether your intake department is keeping your law firm competitive. What do I mean by tracking? You should have a report that indicates the actual time a potential client contacted your law firm and, within that same report, metrics that reveal when your law firm responded to that initial contact. Taking this one step further, you should know your law firm's average response time (during weekdays, weeknights and weekends), which intake specialists responded fastest, and which intake specialists were converting at the lowest and highest rates.

Another way to measure the effectiveness of your intake department is by measuring the time elapsed between when a lead first comes in to your law firm and when an intake specialist promotes that lead to a qualified status, if appropriate. In an ideal world, when a lead comes in by phone, the status of that lead should be promoted to "qualified" or "disqualified" within a few minutes of receiving the call. If your cases are in a "lead" status (and thereby not yet qualified or disqualified) for days or weeks, regardless of whether they came in over the phone or by internet, something is terribly wrong.

Now, I recognize that it isn't possible to qualify *every* personal injury case on the first phone call. For example, cases that involve a claim of medical malpractice may be very complex and take some time and research to qualify. Often, identifying a viable medical malpractice case is a skill that goes beyond most intake specialists' relevant expertise, and that's okay. You can, however, expect a quick turnaround from your intake specialists on more straightforward cases with simple criteria such as slip and fall and car accident cases. If there isn't a quick turnaround on these simpler criteria cases, your intake specialists are probably not making qualification decisions immediately and that's cause for concern.

You can also use metrics to gauge the effectiveness of your marketing efforts. Admittedly, I'm not a marketing expert. However, as an experienced intake consultant, I work with marketing firms regularly. We both speak languages that are results-oriented. We understand that marketing without good intake is a bad recipe for all involved. We also agree that for a law firm to be successful, good marketing is necessary. Marketing is what gets claimants to contact your law firm. And intake is what gets claimants to sign your retainer.

Although intake and marketing should be treated separately, you can use metrics from intake to gauge whether you need to reevaluate your marketing strategies. An important metric in this regard is your *cost per lead*, or CPL. With this metric, you are dividing the amount of money spent on a specific campaign by the number of leads retrieved from that campaign. For example, if you spent $30,000 for one month of marketing, and that marketing resulted in 1,000 leads, your CPL would be $30. This, by itself, doesn't tell you about the quality of the marketing campaign though.

What you really want to know is your law firm's cost per qualified lead (CPQ). (As an aside, many law firms are only judging their marketing efforts based upon their cost per retained lead (CPR), which I believe is somewhat inconclusive, so let's talk about each.) Your CPR tells you how much your law firm paid for each retained case. Again, if you spent $30,000 on a specific marketing campaign and it resulted in two retained cases, then your law firm's CPR would be $15,000. Some law firms might look at this and think their marketing is faulty and may erroneously seek to make changes to their marketing plans as a result. But the above hypothetical doesn't indicate how many cases qualified from that same marketing campaign. Sticking with the same hypothetical, assume the $30,000 marketing campaign yielded 20 qualified leads. Now consider how ineffective your intake process was if only two of those 20 qualified leads were retained. That's why it's important not to judge your intake department by your law firm's CPR alone and, similarly, why it's important to evaluate the CPQ when analyzing the success of a marketing campaign. As explained using the math above, your CPQ asks you to compare the number of leads that qualified to the amount of money your law firm spent on marketing. If you spent $30,000 on a marketing campaign and it resulted in 20 qualified cases, you would have a CPQ of $1,500. I can't opine whether this CPQ is high, average or low for a particular marketing campaign, but I can tell you that it provides your law firm with a benchmark to use when judging your law firm's marketing success.

You can leverage the same numbers above to also judge aspects of your intake process. In this regard, another intake metric I like to review is my Qualified Percentage (QP). The QP tells you what percentage of leads ultimately qualified. If your law firm received 100 leads and 10 qualified, your law firm's QP would be 10 percent. In addition to telling you whether marketing efforts are providing qualified leads, it also allows you to get a sense of whether your law firm's intake qualification criteria is too stringent or loose for any given marketing campaign. If your law firm's QP is low, it means that either your marketing efforts failed to reach the intended claimant population, or your intake qualification standards were too restrictive. If your law firm's QP is high, it means that either your marketing efforts are doing exactly what you hoped for, or your law firm's qualification criteria may be too broad. An efficient and well-run intake department will consider both possibilities before making conclusions and adjusting its marketing efforts or qualification criteria appropriately.

Metrics can also be extremely useful when tracking the cases your law firm refers out to other law firms. I will explore this concept in the next chapter.

The Power Of Referrals

In the modern personal injury world, every law firm should be taking advantage of referrals to the maximum extent permissible under applicable state law. When I say "referrals," I also mean the opportunity to co-counsel on a case. While every state has different requirements for acquiring referral fees, I recommend that every law firm evaluate, where permissible, the possibility of referring cases out to other law firms. In other words, just because a case doesn't fit within your law firm's specific qualification criteria or is not within your law firm's area of expertise, doesn't mean that same case won't fit within another law firm's qualification criteria or area of expertise. If handled correctly, referrals have the potential to be a tremendous source of revenue for your law firm.

But, it's not as simple as referring cases out to just any law firm. Your brand, reputation and fees are at stake. As a result, it's important to conduct due diligence when considering referrals to another law firm to ensure that the other law firm is serving similar clients effectively, appropriately and holding themselves accountable to the same standards you set for your own intake department. You should ensure that the other law firm is responding to your law firm referrals as quickly as possible. To do this, it becomes necessary to hold refer-out law firms accountable by tracking certain metrics on referrals, and asking the following questions:

How long does it take for the refer-out law firm to respond when you send them a lead?

Do they accept live transfers?

Are they qualifying leads on the first phone call?

Are they asking the potential client to do some work prior to retention?

Do they understand the competitive nature of the legal industry?

Are they adequately updating you on the status of the referral?

Are they reciprocating referrals?

What is their conversion percentage(s)?

What is their justification when rejecting a lead?

Ideally, the law firms you partner with should be able to convert your qualified referrals into retained clients as soon as possible. The best-case scenario would be a phone call that your intake department can live transfer to the other law firm who can then acquire a signed retainer while on the call. Here, the call continues, and the potential client retains the other law firm on that first live-transferred phone call. I recognize that this isn't always possible, due to a lack of resources and general understanding of intake, but your law firm should still clearly articulate to the other law firm your expectation that referral cases be reviewed and qualified as soon as possible by the other law firm.

If the refer-out law firm takes their time in reviewing the case, that's undoubtedly going to hurt your law firm. Even though the other law firm would potentially be handling the case, your marketing dollars paid for the lead, and if they squander it, that's a waste of your financial investment. As such, there must be a clear line of communication about the expectations between your law firm and the refer-out law firm. It is similarly important to express your expectations for referral law firms in writing, and request that they sign a referral or co-counsel agreement. This could assist in protecting your referral fee or limiting your potential liability in the future.

Think about this scenario:

> *Your law firm gets a lead from someone who is looking for legal representation in a criminal matter. Since your law firm is strictly a personal injury law firm, you choose to refer the lead out to another law firm that specializes in criminal defense matters. After a review of the facts of the case, the other law firm tells you that it doesn't handle that specific type of criminal matter. Does this mean you should stop trying to refer the lead out? Or should you look for another referral partner?*

Hopefully you guessed correctly. There's nothing wrong with contacting multiple law firms before rejecting a lead. Again, these leads are your marketing dollars at work. *You need to squeeze every ounce of water from the towel before concluding that it's dry.* I can't tell you how many times I've listened to an intake specialist reject a claim because they didn't know of an attorney or law firm who handled the specific type of claim that the claimant called about. *We're better than this*! Let's create the legal relationships. Let's ensure that we don't leave any potential value on the table.

Referrals are an important part of my intake philosophy and make implementing my strategies much easier. If you're able to refer cases that you don't want to other law firms, you can eliminate anxiety about qualifying as many claimants as possible through your intake processes and department. Running a law firm should be about maximizing profit, and every potential roadblock to that goal shouldn't be met with shrugged shoulders or, worse yet, unawareness of lost opportunities that would increase revenue. You should instead tackle these problems head-on, one at a time, and work to figure out how you can eliminate them. In some situations, the obstacle that you once thought was insurmountable just might end up making you money. Sometimes... a lot of money.

Bottom line: Almost every lead contacting your law firm is a lead that you've paid for and you should treat all leads as potentially valuable sources of revenue even if they don't meet your in-house qualification criteria or you don't have the particular expertise in-house. You never know when a lead's neighbor, friend, or co-worker is looking for a recommendation. So, using your best efforts to retain or refer out (where appropriate or necessary) is vital.

The Necessity Of Recording Intake Calls

Now it's time to focus on one of my favorite topics: listening to and assessing the effectiveness of your intake specialists on the phone. I still remember the first time I listened to recordings of my intake specialists as managing attorney. I was literally floored by what I heard. Every call would have benefited from some improvement. And I mean it. Every. Single. Call. To this day, I'm sure it's partly why my hair started to turn gray. That, and how the New York Mets organization is run, but I digress.

Recording the calls between your intake specialists and potential clients is a good way to gauge the effectiveness of your intake department overall and individual staff members, but I caution here because every state has different parameters on if, and how, calls may be recorded. While I swear by the results yielded from listening to intake calls, I strongly advise you to confirm that you are compliant with all applicable state laws regarding telephonic recordings. And that obviously goes for everything written in this book.

Listening to recorded calls is not always pleasant. You learn so much about your intake specialists and how they approach leads, including their personality, their tone, their level of attention, how they respond to questions, if they brag about your law firm, their ability to reassure potential clients about working with your law firm and, of course, everything they get wrong. You'll hear mistakes that your intake specialists have been making for months or years—and you'll kick yourself for not addressing them sooner. Lots of times, the outlines or directives that law firms provide to their intake specialists and think are being followed, are not. And we wouldn't know it if we didn't listen to their calls.

While consulting for law firms, I offer the ability to listen to and assess their intake specialists on the phone. There's one specific recorded call that I listened to that still bothers me to this day. When I talk about cases that keep me up at night, this one is always at the top of my list. The call involved a potential client who had recently been involved in a car wreck. She explained that it had been raining outside, and another vehicle side-swiped her car, causing significant damage and an injury that required immediate hospitalization. The potential client indicated that the police arrived at the scene and placed liability on the other driver. The law firm had everything it needed to qualify and retain a potentially valuable case. It was literally the perfect case, the kind you learn about in law school, and this potential client contacted the law firm seeking legal guidance and representation. What happened next was another reminder of how important it is to properly train intake specialists and assess their individual performance.

The intake specialist clearly and immediately *turned down* the case. Yup, the intake specialist informed the potential client that the law firm was not interested in representing her. The reasoning? The intake specialist thought that since it was a rainy day, the potential client couldn't possibly claim that the other party had liability for the crash even though it was, according to the police, the other party's fault. The intake specialist didn't understand the law—and, because of it, the law firm lost out on an all-but-guaranteed favorable outcome for the claimant as well as for the law firm.

Listening to those first phone calls, if permissible, is like opening the curtains when you wake up in the morning. Sure, you can delay waking up. But at some point, if you want your law firm to be productive and get the day started off on the right foot, opening the curtains is a first step. To truly improve at intake, you must look at what your law firm is doing wrong and be brutally honest about any uncovered deficiencies. This isn't an easy task, but I promise the rewards will be well worth it.

Below is a non-exhaustive list of what I've witnessed intake specialists doing wrong over the phone:

- They sound uninterested.
- They are unresponsive or fail to adequately answer a potential client's questions.
- They sound too robotic.
- They provide the wrong answers.
- They mistakenly disqualify cases.
- They make promises the law firm may not be able to keep.
- They have long hold times.
- They are multi-tasking.
- They are not listening to what the caller is saying.
- They are not conveying an interest to assist the potential client.
- They are not conveying reassurance or empathy.
- They are delaying sign-ups.

Most intake specialists should be able to breeze through conventional cases without issue. It's the more uncommon or unconventional cases that start to cause trouble. If you aren't listening to intake calls, you're missing out on an opportunity to sit down with your intake specialists, discuss mistakes with them and increase productivity. This doesn't have to be a learning opportunity solely for them. If you want to maximize client retention and your law firm's ROI, you should ensure your intake department has a commitment to improvement and perfection the same way you do.

To make sure that you and your law firm's intake specialists are on the same page, you should randomly listen to a certain number of intake calls on a monthly basis. You should also ask yourself if your intake specialists really know what your law firm does or what makes your law firm so valuable to potential clients. This may seem like common sense to an experienced attorney who eats and breathes personal injury law, but will it seem as obvious to an intake specialist who may be having their first experience in the legal world through your law firm? As attorneys, we know that we are, by far, the best plausible option for potential clients who have been injured or otherwise aggrieved and that with our legal representation (as opposed to being *pro se*), we can yield clients on average at least a three and a half times bigger return. *But do your intake specialists know that?*

When listening to recorded intake calls, you may become infuriated. You may be exasperated that your law firm's intake specialists are not picking up on cues that are obvious to you, or that they're not seeing the potentially great case you see. You cannot let that anger carry over into your discussions with intake specialists. Successful law firms should be built on mutual respect between all employees, attorneys and non-attorneys alike.

Presumably, your intake specialist is not making the mistake(s) on purpose. If you dedicate the time to meet with your law firm's intake specialists, explain their mistakes to them and share with them what you do and why it's so important, they are more likely to be receptive, engaged and committed to not repeating the same mistake(s) in the future.

As wrenching and time consuming as it may seem to listen to recorded intake calls (and uncover all the potential cases that may have become lost opportunities for your law firm), it is equally rewarding to sit down *with* your intake specialists and observe them noticing their own mistakes over the phone. I've done this with intake specialists countless times, and I've witnessed so much improvement from some specialists that going forward when listening to their phone calls, I didn't hear any critical mistakes—maybe just a difference in opinion. And that's when you know that your intake specialists are doing their part in maximizing your ROI!

When you know you're going to be held accountable, most people will work hard to meet or exceed expectations. Similarly, when your intake specialists know that you're going to meet with them regularly about their intake calls, they're going to care more about how they handle them. You want your intake department to be a well-oiled machine, but there's a lot of work to do before it's running (and continues to run) smoothly. Substantial time should be dedicated to meeting with intake specialists one-on-one about the importance of intake, their unique mistakes and issues, and both individual and collective ways to improve. Remember, an effective intake department is a main reason your law firm has an opportunity to generate revenue and if you want to maximize productivity, you should be working with intake specialists and listening to their recorded calls on a frequent basis.

In addition to the learning opportunities above, there are a few concepts I recommend teaching all intake specialists before they even pick up your law firm's phone. When intake specialists are on an intake call, they frequently run into something I like to refer to as *softball opportunities*, which are simple chances to engage the potential client and boost the potential client's confidence in your law firm. There are a few frequently asked questions that all intake specialists should have memorized in this regard, such as:

How much is the potential client's case generally worth?

When will the potential client's case resolve?

What does the litigation process entail?

Does your law firm need the potential client to gather any documents?

Your intake specialists should expect to be asked these (and many other) softball questions and should have answers prepared that inspire confidence in your law firm and provide reassurance and clarity to the potential client.

Of course, this level of preparation goes beyond simply answering expected questions. Potential clients seeking personal injury representation are typically going through similar situations. They were just in an accident or otherwise aggrieved, are likely in pain and uncertain about their futures. Many callers are going to be speaking with intake specialists at a vulnerable time in their lives, and intake specialists should be prepared for that. They should show empathy toward the potential client, and a calm competence that communicates that your law firm can handle all their legal needs. Indeed, an intake specialist who balances empathy with a sense of urgency to sign your law firm's retention agreement is immensely valuable to your law firm.

The only thing that's going to get an intake specialist to this point is repetition and constant dialogue. Once your intake specialists have mastered the frequently asked questions and can communicate empathetically, there's still plenty of learning opportunities to have. These opportunities largely come out of leads that are unconventional and not covered in typical training sessions. Maybe the potential client calls in with a less conventional case, such as a medical malpractice case, which is difficult to qualify without more. Maybe the intake specialist is unclear about whether to refer the potential client to another law firm or which other law firm to refer the potential client to. It's impossible for an intake specialist to be prepared for every type of scenario and to know every answer on that first phone call; however, adopting a regular practice of listening to intake calls will facilitate an ongoing learning experience for your intake specialists. And you never know when a teaching opportunity may arise!

Hiring Intake Specialists And Effective Communication

If your law firm is committed to building its own dedicated intake department instead of outsourcing the responsibility, it is important to hire candidates with the right type of personalities and skill sets. For intake specialists to excel, they need to know exactly what they're getting into. In my experience, newer intake specialists tend to burn out quickly because they're rushed and doing the same repetitive functions daily. It is important to recognize that speaking on the phone for as frequently as most intake specialists do could be quite tiresome and, therefore, takes a particular type of personality to thrive.

When reviewing applications, there is no single indicator for who will make a successful intake specialist. Indeed, there are very few prior work experiences that can adequately prepare someone as an intake specialist for a law firm and, although it may sound counterintuitive, prior personal injury experience is *not* the most relevant experience to seek. Rather, in my opinion, the most relevant prior work experience to have is in a role that required sales over the phone or as a customer service representative. Although experience within personal injury law could be helpful, the basic concepts of talking and empathizing with people and trying to sell a service are the same. These jobs put workers on the spot and ask them to be a reassuring and competent solution for potential clients interested in their services. Moreover, you're looking for people who can independently solve problems, although I recognize that independence is something that they'll get even more experience of if hired as an intake specialist.

An intake specialist's personality, coupled with how they sound over the phone, is extremely important for the role and someone's personality can be vastly different on the phone than it is in real life. I recommend scheduling an initial phone interview with applicants before inviting them in to your law firm for an in-person interview. That way, you can appreciate how welcoming and conversational (or not) a prospective intake specialist is in the telephonic environment in which they would be working. You should also make sure that you're hiring positive personalities. In most intake departments, intake specialists work in the same shared spaces all day and interact with each other constantly. Someone with a negative attitude will inevitably filter into the outlook of other intake specialists, eventually affecting the quality of work of the intake department collectively.

I mentioned at the outset that intake specialists tend to burn out quickly. One of the best ways to ensure that new hires are prepared for the demanding role of an intake specialist is to expose them to the type of work they'll be doing every day...*before they are offered a job*. Have prospective intake specialists listen to mock phone calls and sit down with other intake specialists while they are making phone calls and using the law firm's software so they can envision what the role entails. Moreover, this will allow you to observe and assess how the intake specialist reacts to their first taste of the job.

During the interview process, you should communicate to applicants the overall goals of your law firm. Candidates should understand that effective intake is critical to your law firm and that your intake specialists are tasked with making decisions every day that affect every level of your law firm. They also need to appreciate that they will be held accountable, and what your expectations of the role are. In this regard, it is important to communicate: (i) the metrics your law firm uses to track intake performance, such as conversion percentage, response time, and overall phone personality; and (ii) that calls will be recorded, if permissible by state (and the necessity for recording calls). My philosophy is that you shouldn't keep prospective intake specialists in the dark about what would be expected of them, if hired.

Because intake specialists are usually lower-paid workers in your law firm, there might be an expectation among applicants that it's a *typical hourly wage job*—that is, that it's not an essential function to your law firm and there will be a lot of downtime when the phones are quiet. For intake specialists, this couldn't be further from the truth. When law firms have issues with new intake staff, it's almost always because new hires assumed their lower-paid positions weren't essential to the law firm and required minimal, almost robotic-type, effort. This is yet another reason to ensure that you clearly communicate to newly hired (and existing) intake specialists how important their role is, and that you will empower and support them to make reasonable decisions that affect the entire law firm every day.

Of course, there is something that is often overlooked when it comes to the intake responsibilities; that is, how attorneys treat the intake specialists and process, as a whole. Often, situations arise during the intake process that require an intake specialist to interact with attorneys, either to get confirmation before qualifying a particular claim or to answer a legal question. It sounds as strange to write down as it may be to read, but many attorneys have no interest in intake and are completely unaware of their law firm's intake approach or process. In fact, many attorneys hear the word *intake* and turn the other direction, and the reasons are typically that:

1. *Attorneys want to focus on litigating cases and don't perceive themselves to be responsible for, or having involvement in, selling their law firm's services to a potential client.*

2. *In successful law firms, attorneys (perhaps unreasonably) are spoiled with new client matters appearing on their desk regularly, having no idea what the law firm (or intake) did to acquire those new clients.*

In sum, the key to any well-functioning law firm is great communication between all levels of employees. If attorneys are curt the first time an intake specialist asks them a question about a potential client, think about how that may affect that intake specialist the next time a question arises. Is that intake specialist likely to ask the attorney another question or might they just decide it's not worth the law firm's time and reject a potentially valuable claim? I can tell you what I've observed in my experience, but I don't think you'll be happy with my observations. Attorneys should have an open-door policy with intake specialists—and that means every attorney—and there must be an understanding of the value that intake specialists bring to the law firm.

Maintaining Momentum: Assessing Cases Appropriately

To maintain your intake department's momentum, you must be conscious of the obstacles your law firm is likely to run into and be prepared to face them. A substantial number of leads are lost during the intake process because intake specialists are unsure of the status of the lead. Status (or category) refers to the stage a potential case is in (i.e., how far along in the intake process it is). Different stages of a lead require different levels of attention and urgency from your intake specialists.

When a new lead arrives by phone call, it should be treated with the top level of priority and urgency, which means your intake specialist should determine whether the lead qualifies for retention as quickly as possible and, assuming the lead is qualified, diligently work to have the potential client signed. The gold standard here is to have the potential client sign your law firm's retention agreement electronically while still on the phone with your intake specialist. If that's not possible, however, scheduling an in-person sign-up for as soon as possible thereafter (*same day should be the goal*) is the next best option. As the sign-up date and method move further away in time from the potential client's initial outreach to your law firm, the likelihood of retention diminishes.

There should still be a sense of urgency conveyed for cases your intake specialist is unable to have signed electronically while on the phone. For example, maybe a potential client is averse to signing an electronic retention agreement and instead wants to come into the office to sign, in-person, in a few hours. This may seem great at first, but those few hours still afford the potential client time to contact other law firms. This means that during those few hours, the lead still has a high-priority status. There are a couple of things that an intake specialist can do during this time to make the potential client more likely to retain your law firm. For example, an intake specialist could send the potential client a text message stating the following:

> "It was great speaking with you. We're scheduled to meet at our office, at [state address], in two hours. We look forward to getting our investigation started on your behalf!"

If your intake specialist feels the potential client might need a stronger push toward your law firm, another option would be to have the call live-transferred to an attorney within your office. I'd like to discuss this a bit further. I can't tell you how many times law firms inform me that their attorneys have nothing to do with intake. If there's a trend I'm proud to be a strong advocate of, it's this: *Utilize your attorneys more at intake.* This brings us back to that car dealership analogy. Every time I've walked into a car dealership, a manager has approached me. This was the dealership's way of trying to make me feel important and ensure that I didn't walk out of the dealership without a new set of car keys in my hand. Because many law firms are unable, unwilling, or uninterested in having an attorney speak with a potential client, we must consider this as an opportunity to outdo competing law firms. In an ideal world, I would have an attorney speak with every qualified lead. Yup, I said it. *Every. Qualified. Lead.*

It can only help your law firm's chances of being retained. Moreover, it conveys a sense of importance to the potential client, gives your sales pitch more punch and overall reassures the potential client that they did the right thing by contacting your law firm.

Status is also important to the law firms you refer potential clients to. I spoke earlier about holding partnering law firms accountable to the same standard of service you hold your own intake specialists to, and this equally applies to the way referral law firms treat lead status. If you refer a live call out to another law firm, you should expect that law firm to react with a gold standard of service by having someone readily available to receive the transferring call and seamlessly continue the qualification process. If the referral law firm doesn't have someone immediately available to receive the call, you should have a system in place whereby you email the potential client's information to the partnering law firm and give that law firm's information to the potential client so that they're comfortable calling independently. Once you've completed this transfer of information, you should expect the partnering law firm to give the case a high-priority status and work to contact, qualify, and potentially sign that claimant as soon as possible.

Law firms shouldn't have a nonchalant attitude about referral cases and shouldn't cease communicating with potential clients after the initial retention opportunity. Rather, law firms should ensure the potential client is given the status and attention it deserves by the partnering law firm—and that your law firm receives credit for the referral. To do this, your law firm should request that the partnering law firm acknowledge when they receive your referral and contact you at certain stages of their pursuit towards retention. You should ask to be notified once the partnering law firm speaks with the potential client, whether the potential client meets their criteria for qualification and retention, and what their plans are to become retained. If a referred case doesn't meet the partnering law firm's qualification criteria, they should notify you immediately so that your law firm can consider whether to seek to refer the potential client to another law firm.

When debating whether you would like to get more involved in referring cases or are unsure whether it's appropriate to request status touchpoints from partnering law firms who you have referral arrangements with, use a cost-benefit analysis to truly understand how much of a ROI your law firm may receive for fairly minimal effort. Let's use an example:

A potential client contacts your law firm and your intake specialist speaks with her for 5 to 10 minutes before determining the claim doesn't meet your law firm's qualification criteria. They might be calling with a medical malpractice case, for example, which your law firm doesn't specialize in. Your intake specialist then spends another five minutes referring the potential client to another law firm which specializes in the subject matter. If the partnering law firm receives a live call transfer, this is an instantaneous process; if not, your intake specialist will write an email detailing the potential client's case to the partnering law firm, which would take another five minutes.

Based on the above, at most, your intake specialist spent approximately 20 minutes to ultimately refer the potential client to another law firm (and the referral process could certainly be curtailed if your intake/ referral process is streamlined). After that initial referral, your intake specialist would send follow-up emails to the partnering law firm to confirm the referral was received and that the partnering law firm is working diligently to qualify and sign. This shouldn't take more than a few minutes out of your intake specialist's day. And when the matter ultimately (hopefully) resolves, the referral could net your law firm a substantial amount in referral fees for something that required minimal investment of resources.

Apathy plagues many law firms and, as a consequence, substantial revenue is lost. Many law firms believe they're doing fine as is, and the effort or thought that goes into changing their policies and practices doesn't seem worthwhile. Maybe a law firm isn't sure where to start. One time, I consulted with a law firm that had a policy for referring cases but made no effort to track the status of those cases that had been referred. This resulted in the law firm essentially losing track of more than 500 retained cases and quite possibly, the referral fees attributed thereto. Working with that law firm, we tracked down every one of the unaccounted-for referral cases and some of what was discovered shocked me. There were dozens of cases that the partnering law firm never classified as referrals from the originating law firm, and I worked to ensure that my client/law firm received the referral credit it was supposed to.

I've been on the other side of the referral exchange too, having consulted with multiple law firms that sought guidance on how to handle cases that were referred to them. Referred-in cases should be treated as immensely valuable by law firms because they're essentially free. Another law firm invested the time and money in a marketing campaign that motivated the potential client to call, and they just referred the client to your law firm after determining that it didn't meet their law firm's qualification criteria or that the claimant would be better served if your law firm handled the litigation process. The only thing your law firm has to do is be available and respond when the referral is offered. With this in mind, a law firm that receives referral cases should do everything possible, not only to impress and retain the potential client, but also to keep a clear line of communication with the law firm referring the potential client. If you handle referrals professionally and promptly, you're more likely to be sent more referral opportunities in the future and acquire even more *free* cases for just a few minutes of your intake specialist's time to qualify them. *A significant component of any intake department's success is in responding, and referrals are no different.* Going the extra mile to communicate with the potential client and the partnering law firm can take you far, and you'll be amazed at what a drastic difference it will make in your law firm's revenue.

There are several status levels law firms use to categorize a case when intake specialists are following up with a potential client. One of them is the first follow-up phone call for potential clients who contact your law firm through a method other than by phone. If a law firm is unsuccessful after its first attempt to reach the potential client by phone, the law firm must decide how much longer, and how frequently, the law firm wants to follow-up with the potential client before abandoning the lead. I work with law firms regularly to determine the answer to this question, and it varies depending on the type of lead, the resources of the law firm, and the method of contact, among other factors.

After your intake specialist speaks with a potential client, they are likely to move the lead into one of the below general statuses:

1. *Sign-up*
2. *Internal Review*
3. *Referral*
4. *Law Firm Rejection*
5. *Lost Opportunities*

When a case goes into *Sign-Up* status, it means the potential client has agreed to review your law firm's retention agreement (and accompanying documents) either electronically, by mail, or in-person. *The signed retention agreement is so close, you can feel it!* It's critical that your law firm ensures the relationship is nurtured appropriately and that your intake specialist is in constant communication with the potential client, while also considering the possibility of bringing in an attorney and conveying a sense urgency to retain. Too many law firms detrimentally believe that, by scheduling an in-person sign-up, or emailing or mailing the law firm's retention documents, the potential client is *certain to retain the law firm*. The law firm is forgetting (or not aware) that the potential client is still a free-agent (to use a sports term) who has likely contacted multiple law firms and has likely received multiple retainer agreements. The sooner law firms accept this reality, the better their conversion percentages will be.

Note that sometimes a potential client asks to be called back on a certain date or at a certain time, maybe because they don't want to make a retention decision without speaking to their significant other or they are at work and unable to discuss details freely and openly. This isn't at all ideal for a law firm, but it doesn't matter. If a potential client requests to be called back at a certain date or time, your intake specialist should be scheduling to call then, down to the very minute.

Intake specialists sometimes fall into a trap of not prioritizing the date and time of an in-person sign-up, and that's a big issue from my perspective. Your intake specialists should aim to sign potential clients imminently, same day if possible, and not look to postpone and procrastinate the retention by deferring potential clients a few days or weeks out. A related issue that many law firms experience when trying to sign clients involves what the intake specialist communicates in the scheduling process. For example, I've heard intake specialists say the following to potential clients:

We have an opening on Wednesday at 3:00 pm.

I'll have one of our investigators contact you about a date and time to meet.

Can you come in to our office tomorrow?

Can you see the passive trend above? None of these statements focus on the earliest availability of the potential client. *Law firms should always focus on the potential client's availability while conveying a sense of urgency.* Instead of the above, encourage your intake specialists to employ language such as the following when scheduling an in-person sign-up:

We can have someone available at your earliest convenience today, whether it's in our office, your home, or any other preferred location. We can even walk you through an electronic sign-up while we are speaking with you right now. Since we are unable to begin our investigation until you retain our services, and because we would like to start working on your behalf immediately, time is certainly of the essence. What's the earliest time you can be available today?

When you speak with a potential client who satisfies your qualification criteria but who requests to schedule an in-person sign-up, your intake specialist should offer to have someone meet the potential client—with all the necessary paperwork—within a few hours' time. You can't afford the lapse of time it would take to check the availability of the person(s) who would hold the in-person sign-up, whether it is an attorney or third-party investigator, before offering to meet the potential client. This is an industry that must revolve around becoming retained immediately to thrive. The potential ROI that personal injury cases have is too significant to wait for the potential client to come to you. You might be able to sign *some* clients with this mentality, but you'll miss out on many others who will find another law firm that will come to them and work around their schedule.

Bottom line: If your law firm can't meet the needs of a potential client in our culture of instant gratification, the client will find another law firm that can. As such, as soon as a qualified claimant shows interest in your law firm, you should express interest in immediately beginning an investigation and work to get the potential client off the market.

The next status—*Internal Review*—is one that all law firms should strive to avoid. An Internal Review is the non-committal, kicking-the-can-down-the-road status that sabotages so many cases before they even begin. An Internal Review is when the intake specialist is unable to determine whether the potential client meets the law firm's qualification criteria for retention, telling the potential client instead that they'll review their claim internally and get back to them shortly. Having to call a potential client back is the death knell of intake. It communicates that either you're not as interested in their case as you should be, or, even worse, that you're not competent enough to know whether you can assist in their matter. Either way, the moment the potential client gets off the phone with you, they are likely to contact another law firm who may provide an enthusiastic and definite response.

Whenever I consult with law firms and see the Internal Review status being utilized, I work hard to eliminate the status completely from their tracking systems. Not only is Internal Review a massive turn-off for any potential client, but it's also a waste of valuable law firm time and resources. Every intake department should be well-equipped, prepared, and empowered to make a determination as to whether to sign or refer a case. The minute your law firm stops using the Internal Review status is the minute you'll begin seeing real improvement in your intake department.

The last status that I would like to discuss in this chapter is *Law Firm Rejection*. This is exactly what it sounds like: when a law firm cannot qualify a potential claim, it will reject the claim and forgo an opportunity to be retained. At first glance, you would think this status is self-explanatory. But, as an industry, we must begin to understand that mistakes have been made and will continue to be made. Unless we look for the mistakes, we won't know how to fix them. Time and time again, I help law firms realize that they may be rejecting claims that have *real value*. And the only way to determine which of these rejected claims have value is to review every lead that the law firm has generated regardless of whether it was rejected or accepted. Yes. *Every. Single. Lead.*

There are many assumptions I made in writing this book. One assumption is that law firms use software to track each of its leads. Additionally, I assumed that law firms are tracking, to some extent, the status of each of its leads. One assumption I have not made is that most law firms are reviewing every lead that it generated to ensure the correct decision was made. Unfortunately, I know the opposite to be true. If you want to start maximizing your law firm's ROI (from marketing campaigns or otherwise), begin by inspecting the results of every lead your law firm acquired. I promise it will be worth your time.

Since we've already discussed the status of *Referrals* in this and proceeding chapters, let's next explore a status that requires a chapter of its own: *Lost Opportunities.*

Handling Lost Opportunities; Accountability

It's important to understand this concept: *No matter how efficient your intake department may be, it's impossible to sign every case your law firm wants.* Potential clients may either lose interest, stop returning phone calls, or retain another law firm. A good intake department will understand this concept and not grow frustrated by it or, worse yet, make excuses for why the case wasn't signed or disclaim the case as not being a desirable one anyway. Rather, a good intake department will use these lost (retention) opportunities as learning experiences—that is, as motivation to examine the potential clients that were lost and strive to understand the possible reason(s) behind it. They'll also work hard to hold themselves accountable if certain intake metrics fall below your law firm's expectations or goals.

One of the simplest ways you can improve your law firm's intake is by determining *why* your intake department lost opportunities to become retained. Through my years of experience and consultations with law firms, I've begun compiling a non-exhaustive list of the common reasons and patterns that cause law firms to miss out on retention opportunities. Below are my top ten reasons (in no particular order):

1. *Inadequate response time*
2. *Inadequate follow-up attempts*
3. *Inability to qualify a claim on the first phone call*
4. *Inability to retain while on the first phone call*
5. *Inability to schedule sign-ups for the same day*
6. *Lack of attorney involvement*
7. *Lack of management*
8. *Lack of accountability*
9. *Poor hiring practices*
10. *Inability to convey interest and a sense of urgency*

The best thing your law firm can do is track the reasons for the lost opportunities to become retained. That way, you can identify where your intake department's weaknesses lie, whether it is with individual intake specialists or the intake department as a unit (or a combination of both). Moreover, I recommend that law firms review their intake department's statistics regularly, preferably daily, so that any (repeated) mistakes may be uncovered and rectified as soon as possible. For example, law firms should analyze how many leads come in each day; of those leads, how many were qualified by an intake specialist; and, of the leads that qualified, how many were signed. This will give your law firm an idea of the results from any marketing campaigns that are running. As importantly, it will create a regular process for reviewing which cases were not (yet) signed and will help to mitigate any lost opportunities to sign. It's inevitable that intake specialists will make mistakes and, unless someone is committed to looking at the statistics and ensuring that right decisions are made, your intake department will likely keep repeating the same mistakes.

In the personal injury world, I've worked as a litigating attorney, managing attorney, founding partner of a law firm, intake consultant, and CEO of an outsourced intake department. These experiences have taught me that the most important trait every successful business and employee should have is *accountability*. Managers should be held accountable for the policies and protocols they implement, and staff should be held accountable for the way they execute those policies and protocols. In order to hold employees accountable, however, you must review your expectations and goals with employees and departments as a whole and work together to make improvements when expectations and goals are not achieved.

There are a few common reasons employees don't meet expectations. Maybe the employee lacks the skills necessary to meet the standards established for them. Maybe the employee's responsibilities weren't clearly articulated. Or maybe the employee is unaware of what they would be held accountable for. Too many times, managers establish rules or protocols, ask employees to follow them, and carelessly assume that this is sufficient to obtain success. It's not! Rules and protocols must be clearly articulated and revisited frequently to reinforce the importance of achieving certain standards and expectations—and should be changed when the rules or protocols are no longer effective.

There will be occasions when your intake specialists are unable to make qualification decisions on a potential case and will need to consult with an attorney. While your intake specialists will understand the importance of becoming retained as soon as possible, attorneys are often unaware of the time sensitivity in intake and won't review potential cases with the same sense of urgency. To have an effective intake process, you must not only hold your intake specialists accountable, but you must also hold the people they speak with, including attorneys, accountable. You must clearly establish, to all levels of your law firm, that signing qualified claimants is a top priority, and time is of the essence in the qualification and retention process.

We must also hold our third-party vendors accountable to provide the best services possible. If you employ an answering service to assist potential clients after business hours on weeknights and over weekends, you need to clearly establish with the answering service when, and to whom, to live transfer potential clients to. If you see potential leads call in that should have been live transferred by the answering service but weren't, you must make the answering service aware of their mistake.

If your law firm utilizes outside investigators to assist with potential client sign-ups, they must also be held accountable. I've seen behavior from investigators across different law firms that simply baffles me. Investigators that are hired to meet with potential clients and effectuate retention on your law firm's behalf shouldn't have the ability to reschedule sign-ups because the time wasn't convenient for them. Clearly articulate to investigators the expectation that they should work around the potential client's schedule, not their own. By communicating this expectation and evaluating whether the investigators are meeting it, you can help avoid some lost opportunities in retention.

And most importantly, you must hold intake specialists accountable. They are the lifeblood of your business and from the moment they answer your phone to the moment they have potential clients execute a retention agreement, they are the individuals who put your law firm in the best position to earn and increase revenue. You must establish very clear responsibilities for them and ensure that each intake specialist knows what the expected conversion percentages are for your law firm, how often they should be following-up with potential clients, and what methods they should be using to accomplish both.

Accountability, though, isn't just about managing employees and third-party vendors; you must strive to be accountable to potential clients as well. When a potential client contacts your law firm, they're expecting you to be able to reassure them of their concerns—and help them navigate seamlessly through the intimidating legal process. If you market your law firm as being readily available 24 hours a day, seven days a week, you must be prepared to sign potential clients or explain the legal process to them at 10:00 pm on a Saturday evening. If you ask potential clients to reschedule a call or aren't enthusiastic on the phone, then you aren't holding your law firm accountable to the expectations of the potential client. To truly maximize your ROI, you must offer services that competing law firms are unwilling to offer, services that might seem unnecessary at first glance. The strongest cases can come through in the middle of the night and if a human being answers the phone, you're already putting your law firm in a position of advantage against other law firms who only have an answering machine available at that hour.

I've lost count of the number of times I've spoken to potential clients at unexpected, off hours, over the weekend or late at night, and they were astonished each time to hear my voice. I exceeded their expectations and was almost always retained as a result. Being readily available can only help a law firm in retention, and those of us in the personal injury world should quickly abandon the mentality of operating a business between the hours of 9:00 am and 5:00 pm, Monday through Friday. If you want to remain accountable to potential clients, your law firm should be available whenever, and however, a potential client contacts you for legal assistance.

Intake Options For Your Law Firm

I apply the concepts and strategies described in this book within my own companies: Maximum Intake Consulting, Inc. (Max Intake) and ICE. At Max Intake, I consult law firms regularly on ways to improve all aspects of their intake department and process. This includes developing, implementing and enhancing a law firm's intake by focusing on the procedures, people, and methods of tracking in their intake processes. I also created ICE, which I endearingly refer to as "a call center on steroids", with partners of an intake software company. ICE is a fully functioning outsourced intake department, ready-made for law firms struggling with, or uninterested in undertaking to perform, the intake responsibilities.

The Need For ICE

A problem with traditional call centers is that their staff answer your calls and take messages. Your law firm still must undertake the task of following up with, and qualifying, the potential client. As a result, there may be significant time that passes between when the call is answered and when the call may be qualified and/or signed. This delay provides more than enough time for the claimant to seek other viable law firm options.

In today's competitive legal environment, this time delay is no longer acceptable. Your law firm must strike while the iron is hot, and traditional call centers that are used for intake are antithetical to that need in many ways. Make no mistake about it—I fully support the use of a call center and the need to outsource certain calls to them; however, when it comes to intake and the response to new leads, the industry needs more.

Conceptually, ICE was created as a call center that completely removed the time delay between when a new lead contacted your law firm and when the lead was ultimately qualified and signed. We achieve this by giving ICE and its intake specialists the same level of authority I implore you to give your own intake specialists. At ICE, we aim to retain potential clients on that first phone call, just like the best intake departments do. ICE has been immensely successful, in large part because we do what many law firms don't have the resources, time, or initiative to do. Our staff is heavily trained to answer, qualify, follow-up, and sign as well as, or even better than, most law firms do themselves. And we do so by following the guidelines recommended in this book.

One of my favorite stories at ICE involved retaining a qualified case that ICE followed-up with for more than seven months. How many law firms can say they've done this? Certainly only a few, if any. Does that mean that our intake specialist called for seven months until the potential client was ready to speak with us? Of course not! We created a relationship with the potential client and patiently, yet persistently, continued to follow-up. How gratifying will it be when this client receives an award or settlement due to our efforts? And how great will it be when the retained law firm earns a fee from our hard work? Persistence and hard work prevailed again.

With ICE, we've proven that the intake concepts and strategies discussed within this book not only work, but produce results that far exceed the status quo. To accomplish this, ICE takes control of every single aspect of the intake process. Our technology allows us to know exactly which law firm the potential client sought to contact and can support both inbound and outbound marketing campaigns for law firms of all sizes. Most of these law firms are already outsourcing marketing and engaged marketing firms to run campaigns on their behalf. ICE then handles the entire intake process, from the inbound response and qualification, to the follow-up and the eventual client retention for the law firm. And we provide daily reports of the status of every lead to all our law firm clients. Again, it comes back to accountability.

Now, some law firms don't need a company that takes care of the entire intake process. Many high-volume law firms already have a large and well-established intake department that can easily handle inbound campaigns themselves. ICE can still prove beneficial to these law firms because even an established intake department will eventually stop following up, whether on qualified leads that stopped responding or leads that were not yet qualified. For those law firms, we offer to take over the follow-up efforts on those leads. ICE has worked on many marketing campaigns like these for larger law firms—taking over the follow-up efforts on potential leads the law firm assumed were uninterested—and converting them into retained clients. ICE has even been successful with converting leads that were more than one year old into retained clients.

In creating ICE, our company set out to prove that as an industry, we don't have the best practices, and it directly affects the success of a law firm's marketing campaigns, revenue, and margins. Attorneys who outsource their intake to ICE, in whatever form, can focus on what they went to law school for, and we can do what I've spent years of my professional legal career scrutinizing over. Given the potential ROI for personal injury cases, law firms should be doing everything in their power to ensure that their intake departments and processes are operating efficiently and that their results are maximized. We should all appreciate that there's always more money that can be earned, and sometimes that money can be substantial. And that's why ICE has been so successful for its law firm clients.

Below are just a few of the scenarios that should motivate you to partner with ICE:

You're a small to mid-sized law firm that is interested in embarking on a high-volume marketing campaign, but you don't have adequate resources in-house to handle the intake process and you want to maximize your marketing campaign results.

You're a large-sized law firm that acquires a significant number of leads and you realize that your intake specialists are only following up on cases for a minimal or infrequent period and you want to ensure that you haven't rejected or neglected any qualified leads that could have value.

You're a marketing firm that believes your law firm's intake department is not successfully retaining qualified leads.

You're about to open your own law firm and have no experience or interest in handling the intake process in-house.

Regardless of the reasons, if you are thinking about outsourcing any of your law firm's intake responsibilities, ICE should be at the top of your list.

Ride the Wave—Don't Be Swept Away!

I've always prided myself on being an independent thinker and problem solver. I can't stand inefficiency and I don't like when problems are ignored. It took me some time before I realized the inefficiencies and lost opportunities that hinder personal injury law firms because I viewed the legal field with a different lens. As a newly admitted attorney, I viewed the practice of law as simply providing a legal service to clients and solely concerned myself with managing the cases I was assigned and aiming to achieve the best possible outcome for each one of them. And that's certainly a significant part of being a personal injury attorney—and a big reason why I love practicing in this field of law. But to provide legal services to injured or otherwise aggrieved parties, law firms need to be able to sustain themselves as a viable business as well.

It wasn't until I became more involved with intake that I started to see the pervasive problems that plague personal injury law firms. As attorneys, it's easy to lock ourselves in ivory towers and remain unaware of the inner workings of other aspects of a law firm. We don't realize that, at its core, personal injury remains a business. After transitioning from managing attorney of a law firm's intake department to consulting law firm clients on intake, I only became more convinced that the intake process, in general, was broken. Many law firms don't realize the inefficiencies and unknowing mistakes embedded in their law firm's intake process and often avoid the time and resources necessary to fix the problem(s). After all, if a law firm is making money and signing clients, what could be broken?

There's always a moment in meetings with law firm clients when an attorney turns to me with an epiphany and says something like the following: "Gary, do you have any idea how many cases I've lost because of this one thing you're telling me about right now?" And by the conclusion of my law firm consultation, I always turn back to that same attorney with a reassuring voice and communicate that there's no benefit to looking back, frustrated about lost retention opportunities; the experience should be one of learning and that learning should never stop—it should just motivate your law firm to constantly improve and evolve.

In my opinion, law firms with broken intake departments and processes only continue to exist today because so many peer law firms have yet to prioritize their intake. This won't last forever. As time goes on, an increasing number of law firms will realize how important intake is to the viability of their law firm, and they'll begin making the requisite changes and improvements to respond faster, qualify better, follow up more frequently, and sign more clients. Eventually, the pool of clients will start to shrink for law firms that neglect to establish accountability and intake responsiveness as pillars of their law firm. You can get on this wave now or you can be swept away by the current. The power to maximize your law firm's ROI and remain viable in a competitive legal market, is entirely up to you!

About the Author: Gary P. Falkowitz, Esq.

As the President of Maximum Intake Consulting, Inc. (www.maxintake.com), Gary advises law firms, attorneys, and legal organizations on the importance of creating, utilizing, managing and maximizing the legal intake process when communicating with potential clients. He has worked with managing partners, associates, paralegals, and all other support staff in establishing and/or improving their legal intake procedures and processes thereby effectively, and in almost every case significantly, increasing their law firm's conversion percentages. Gary creates customized programs to improve leadership, time management, project management, delegation, prospective client relations and sales skills.

As the CEO of Intake Conversion Experts, LLC (www.intake.law), Gary oversees a staff of intake specialists that represent law firms nationwide at the intake level. The efficiency with which ICE is able to respond, qualify, follow-up and retain clients provides an outsourced solution for any law firm interested in immediate growth.

Gary earned his Bachelor of Arts degree from Brandeis University in 2002 and his Juris Doctorate from St. John's University School of Law in 2005, where he served as a member of the Senior Board of the Moot Court Honor Society. Upon graduating from law school, Gary served as an Assistant District Attorney at the Kings County District Attorney's Office where he focused on the prosecution of criminal matters. Thereafter, he transitioned to the private sector, representing hospitals and doctors against medical malpractice claims at the law firm of Martin, Clearwater and Bell LLP. In 2009, Gary began representing injured claimants at Parker Waichman LLP. He was quickly promoted to a Managing Attorney role within the law firm where he was responsible for managing the law firm's intake department, increasing its' conversion percentages and establishing/growing referral business relationships, among other responsibilities.

Through his years of legal experience, Gary has realized that implementing strong internal procedures and processes, responsiveness (response time) and accountability are three of the most important factors to ensure success and maximize efficiency in legal intake. It doesn't hurt that his passion for the subject matter is unrivaled. In short, Gary believes that the key to maximizing a law firm's revenue is strongly dependent upon the ability to appropriately prioritize and adequately scrutinize at the intake level.

Gary is based in Long Island, New York, but travels regularly based upon client needs. He is married to Lynne, the love of his life and his best friend. Lynne and Gary are the proud parents of three wonderful children: Ethan, Landon and Reese. Currently, Gary serves as the Principal Owner at The Falkowitz Law Firm, PLLC and as a Village Prosecutor in East Hills, New York.

Made in the USA
Coppell, TX
17 October 2023

22996158R00066